TWELVE VOICES TELL THE BLOODY TRUTH

FEIWEL AND FRIENDS
NEW YORK

ARISLEYDA DILONE

ANN FRIEDMAN

MADAME GANDHI

SANTINA MUHA

INGRID NILSEN

period

WILEY READING

ASHLEY REESE

KYLYSSA SHAY

AMINATOU SOW

EMMA STRAUB

JENNIFER WEISS-WOLF

ELIZABETH YUKO

TWELVE VOICES TELL THE BLOODY TRUTH

EDITED BY KATE FARRELL

A FEIWEL AND FRIENDS BOOK
An Imprint of Macmillan Publishing Group, LLC
175 Fifth Avenue, New York, NY 10010

Our books may be purchased in bulk for promotional, educational, or
business use. Please contact your local bookseller or the Macmillan Corporate
and Premium Sales Department at (800) 221-7945 ext. 5442 or by e-mail at
MacmillanSpecialMarkets@macmillan.com.

Library of Congress Cataloging-in-Publication Data is available.
ISBN 978-1-250-14194-1

Book design by Liz Dresner
Feiwel and Friends logo designed by Filomena Tuosto
First edition, 2018
10 9 8 7 6 5 4 3 2 1
fiercereads.com

I first got my period when I was twelve the day my father died

at least I knew what it was, some girls didn't then

we were told you can't go swimming but don't you wanna have

       children

so much for confessionalism

I won't call on the moon like in a real poem

or anthropology or the bible or talk about being untouchable

or power etc. I've nothing at all to say but to exercise

my freedom to speak about everything

—BERNADETTE MAYER

CONTENTS

Introduction

This book grew out of a conversation. We were about half a dozen people in a room, of all different ages and backgrounds and life experiences, but we were all people whose lives were impacted by periods, and we shared an overwhelming desire to talk about them. We were sick of pretending periods didn't happen, and we were excited by the increase in open discussion on the subject.

Periods are in the news and on podcasts and all over the Internet. Movements are growing to repeal state luxury taxes on menstrual products, and to provide supplies for menstruating people who can't access them reliably, both here in the United States and across the globe.

Pop culture is increasingly referencing periods. On BuzzFeed alone, you can read about "9 Types of Periods Anyone Who's Had a Period Will Recognize," or check out "37 Period Memes to Make You Laugh While Losing Ounces of Your Own Blood." And there is a BuzzFeed Period Quiz, of course. I took it and I only got 11 out of 17 right. But here I am writing an introduction to a book about periods! It's a big subject and we can all keep learning, no matter how much period experience we've had.

If I do some rough calculations and

subtract the months that pregnancy and breastfeeding gave me a break from them, I have had at least 432 periods in my life. And it is only very recently that I've begun to feel some lifting of the culture of secrecy and shame surrounding them.

When I was thirteen, my mother had to have a private word with me about getting blood on the toilet seat. I said that there was no way in the world that could possibly have been me. I would never do such a thing. But she knew, somehow, that I had done it, and she even knew how. She said that I must have been letting my tampons thunk against the seat when I took them out. Oh, I wanted to die, because that was exactly what I did. I wanted to see what was on them, so I could know how bad it was, how messy and how much. I felt so ashamed. My sloppy, bloody, grotesque ways had been noticed, pointed out, and condemned. I know my family wasn't trying to shame me. They were just in the camp of Let's Not Have Blood or Other Bodily Fluids on the Toilet Seat We All Have to Share. I'm in that camp, too! But I had already been infected by the larger culture of period shaming. I was mortified that I'd left a trace of my blood somewhere for other people to see. I felt that there was basically *nothing* more disgusting I could have done. To this day, four-hundred-plus periods later and counting, I still think about this every time I change a tampon.

The shame surrounding periods is not just old-fashioned, it is damaging. Menstruation stigma is a global human rights issue. When people who menstruate don't have the means to safely manage their periods, when they don't have access to supplies, or to bathrooms where they feel safe, they miss out on education and the opportunities it leads to.

All societies suffer when half their populations have their educational and economic potential cut short.

We have gathered twelve voices in this book, speaking out on the subject of periods from varied points of view. Arisleyda Dilone writes about the period that never came, and how she has grown to embrace her intersex body and identity. Ann Friedman and Aminatou Sow have the kind of back-and-forth about periods that only two of the smartest, funniest, wisest, and most wonderful best friends could have. Madame Gandhi shares the experience of, and motivations behind, her headline-making free-bleeding London Marathon. Santina Muha tells us what is different, and not different, about coping with a period when you're in a wheelchair. Ingrid Nilsen writes about a trio of period firsts. Wiley Reading helps us understand that men can have periods, too. Ashley Reese writes about the extra layers of difficulty periods can bring for black girls. Kylyssa Shay shows us the reality of coping with periods for homeless people, and shares some ways we might help. Emma Straub describes living for years with the kind of period that means never being too far from a bathroom, ever. Jennifer Weiss-Wolf writes about the politics of periods, and tells us how we can all seize this moment to fight for menstrual equity. And Elizabeth Yuko looks at the progress we have made through the lens of pop culture. These twelve voices each bring a unique perspective to the subject of periods, and all their pieces are illuminating. I hope that readers will find, as all of us who have worked on this project together have found, some parts of this book to recognize and identify with, and other parts that are new and enlightening.

Each of these writers has inspired us, and we hope they will inspire you, too. In seeking out contributors on this subject, we have tried to cover as many different perspectives as possible, within the limited scope of twelve voices. We could have twelve-hundred voices, and we still wouldn't cover the many different ways that periods affect people. But we hope this book will be part of a liberating and ongoing conversation.

—Kate Farrell

TWELVE VOICES TELL THE BLOODY TRUTH

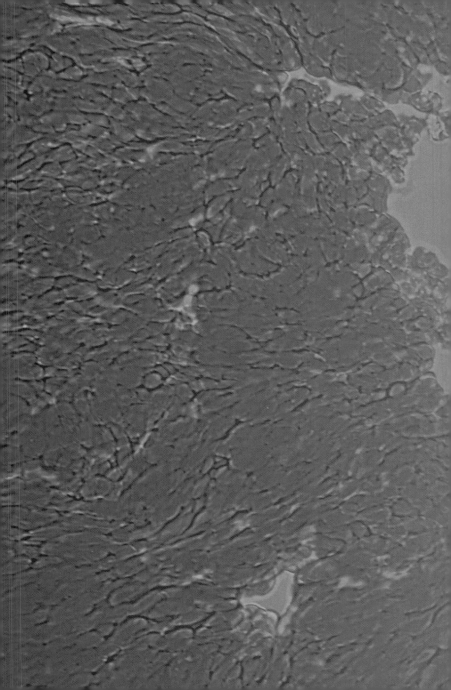

She'll Become a Woman Later

ARISLEYDA DILONE

I am a woman with male chromosomes. This means I never developed breasts or experienced menstruation but nonetheless I was raised as a woman.

Nothing about my appearance ever led others to believe that I was anything but a girl.

As a child, my personality seemed unique only when I compared myself to the girls in my family. Unlike my sisters, I was a proud *marimacho* who loved sports, was obsessed with *The Simpsons*, and would find any reason to stay in school longer. By middle school, my womanhood was a playful deceit propped up by benign teenage lies. I would pretend to have my period so I could skip math class and stare aimlessly out the bathroom window. I knew plenty of girls who lied about getting their period. Sitting in the stall, I would think about bleeding and what it would feel like. While my classmates awaited their periods, I remembered my first encounter with menstruation.

When I was nine, one of my older sisters, Nana, got her period. When Nana and our eldest sister, Rosa, locked themselves in the bathroom, I banged on the door, demanding to know what was happening. Rosa opened the door and proudly announced, "Nana is a woman now." Nana was ten. She showed me some underwear and the bathroom was smelly. I thought the whole situation was gross and I walked away, shaking my head, saying to myself, *That is definitely not happening to me.* And it never did.

It wasn't until my ninth-grade biology class that I began to pay more attention to lessons about female puberty. A very pregnant Mrs. Cox lit up her overhead projector and began a lesson on the menstrual cycle.

"Menstruation is a magical process that connects women to the moon, to the tides, to the earth, to humanity, and to the very essence of the creation of life," she said out of the side of her mouth with a snarky sarcasm.

This explanation seemed interesting but

was just as difficult to grasp as the scientific wording in our textbook. While I was quietly conscious of the fact that I was a fifteen-year-old girl who had yet to get a period, I was mostly uninterested. After all, this didn't seem to apply to me.

Instead I found myself daydreaming about Julio—the new student from the Dominican Republic, the same place I came from. Julio was tall, dark, lanky, and played baseball. We had similar builds. He spoke broken English and struggled to understand the lessons, so I helped him. I wanted to impress him, so I paid close attention. All of a sudden, hereditary traits and Mendel's peas experiment captured my attention. Which parent gave me what features? My mother thought I was a late bloomer like her. At that time my own *Dominicaness* was often on my mind. I am the last in my family to immigrate to the

United States from a rural village in Santiago, Dominican Republic. The village Boca de Bao is a lush green hilly *campo* with dusty dry valleys, dirt roads, and unreliable electricity.

In Bao, adulthood for a young girl began at menstruation. My mother's menstruation was a long-awaited turning point in her life.

My parents met as young teenagers collecting water from a well. And it was love at first sight. Although they wanted to run away as soon as possible, they waited until my mother began her menstruation cycle. Devout from an early age, as a teen she was already *una mujer seria* and my father was just a joyful farm boy. But she was also a late bloomer. She prayed for her period as she watched her younger sisters marry their suitors. Shortly after turning eighteen, she got her period and they eloped.

In the eighties there was an exodus from

my village toward New York City and New Jersey. When my mother was three months pregnant with me, my father left Bao and headed for New York through Mexico. Then, when I was eleven months old, my mother followed. Leaving me and my two older sisters to be raised by the village of extended relatives: great-aunts, grandparents, and cousins. In February 1989, when I was seven years old, I arrived in Long Island, New York, in the middle of a major blizzard. My upbringing in this middle-class suburban port town provided me with options.

Very early on, I recognized that many of the things deemed feminine in my family were optional. Sometimes I opted in and sometimes I opted out. Sometimes I was met with confrontation and sometimes I wasn't. By the age of fifteen my reasoning was: If I didn't get a period, if I didn't have breasts, and yet was still considered a woman, then to some extent my gender identity was up to me. But I enjoyed being a woman. Breasts are an obsession in my family. Women sit around and talk about the size of their breasts and the surgeries they would have. Consequently, I was desperately desirous of breasts. Throughout high school I wore falsies.

In my junior year of high school my mother took me to see an endocrinologist and I opted to begin hormone therapy. I was willing to get a period if it meant getting breasts. So, like my mother many years before me, I found myself constantly waiting to bleed. Unbeknownst to me, behind closed doors and in church pews, my mother was also praying for blood. While I was thinking about breasts, she was thinking about my future, and whether I would become a mother.

All these biological processes occur with an end goal of procreation. Reproduction is entrenched in our identities. I have five siblings. On my mother's side I have nine aunts, one of whom has ten children. All three of my sisters have kids. Today, I have seven nephews and five nieces. My body exists outside of the biological development processes explained in my science class.

Like a voyeur, I stood in the wings watching the women sympathize about a present and future role that didn't include me. I watched as they commiserated over experiences, some of which I didn't want but thought were inevitable. But I knew I wasn't quite one of them because although they made room for me, they did so within a complicit silence. A silence that contained my atypical body. A silence that cradled the ongoing abuse inflicted on their bodies. An abuse that I witnessed but for some reason was spared, leading me to believe I was somehow privileged.

In my senior year of high school I was told my body produced negligible levels of both estrogen and testosterone. And that any sexual development I was experiencing, like height growth and pubic hair, was catalyzed by other hormones. For example, on average, follicle-stimulating hormone (FSH) in an eighteen-year-old girl is 3. My FSH levels were 112. My non-sex developmental hormones were working overtime. But after a year on synthetic progestin and estrogen, my body was still not reacting.

In college, I wanted to be desired. I went full force into appearing as feminine as possible. Straightening my long black hair, wearing makeup and pink from head to toe, I received newfound attention from men.

When I would talk about my body, desirability was a major factor. The fact that I hadn't begun a period was easy to share. It didn't turn men off and most of my female friends expressed some degree of envy. *So you've never had a period? So you can't get pregnant? Lucky! You don't ever have to worry.* On the other hand, I rarely shared that I didn't have breasts and that I was wearing falsies.

During spring break of my freshman year, I underwent surgery. When they operated, they found that one of my ovaries was more like testes tissue, and the other ovary was streaked, meaning neither ovary produced eggs. My uterus was an unformed mass that would never carry children. I would never menstruate even with synthetic hormones. And rather than the oophorectomy that was planned, they performed a complete hysterectomy.

A week later I was back at school.

Senior year of college, I was introduced to Gloria E. Anzaldúa. Anzaldúa was a Chicana feminist, queer, lesbian, writer, farm laborer, and academic. Due to a rare uterine formation, Anzaldúa began to menstruate at five years old. She recalls how her mother made special cloth underwear to soak up the blood. By the age of eight she had developed breasts, about which she says *otras muchachitas no tenían*. She recalls looking at the cloth diapers being hung up on the clotheslines. Only she and her mother knew about her body. This ritual of deep complicit silence between her and her mother hid Anzaldúa's body so well that they both had forgotten it even occurred the way it did.

Anzaldúa changed me. She spoke to my stratified existence as a queer immigrant living in the United States. She spoke to a core silence filled with all parts of me. Suddenly femininity and masculinity became ephemeral. And gender was a distraction to the omnipresent me. The me that shines beyond all gendered things but can be felt through my gaze.

My queer gaze distanced me from the gender-based reproductions of the clan. Anzaldúa's stories of finding strength through her *mestizaje* fed my *campesina* soul. Like Anzaldúa, I am a storyteller in my family. I observe, ponder, and mull over our generations of stories. The depth of her writing taught me so much so quickly. After reading Anzaldúa, I concluded that menstruation exists on a spectrum. That all bodies are like fractals with never-ending layers, spectrums within spectrums. In many ways my body exists on its own terms: Womanhood without breasts. Womanhood without a period.

Womanhood without biological mother-hood. My femininity lies beyond the pre-scribed womanhood. My body expands the boundaries of gender and dismantles the binary simply by existing. But I've hardly had to say any of these things, because my gaze said it all.

When I first started researching intersex bodies I came across a lot of transgender groups. In these groups I encountered new-found parallels within the process of transi-tioning. Hearing trans men talk about their relationship to their breasts and menstru-ation helped me understand that I could exist without breasts and be loved. Trans women reaffirmed my singular womanhood when I would read their expressions of the same yearning for breasts that permeated my youth. No matter the point of view, I stood in certain privilege. Unlike many from the trans community at that point in my life, health insurance had covered my breast augmentation.

MY FEMININITY LIES **BEYOND** THE PRESCRIBED WOMANHOOD. MY BODY **EXPANDS** THE BOUNDARIES OF GENDER AND DISMANTLES THE BINARY **SIMPLY BY EXISTING**.

When I came across the intersex community I fell in love with our vastly different experiences. But I also learned of all the surgeries that had been performed on our bodies without our consent as children. I understood that in many ways I have been fortunate. I didn't undergo genital mutilation as a child. These surgeries are still an ongoing occurrence on intersex bodies all over the world, including the United States.

This body has presented me with options—regarding my presentation, regarding my gender role, regarding my sexuality—and created an opportunity for me to create my own path in this life. Existing as an intersex person has pervaded all facets of my life. At first it was a little secret that manifested in a cheeky smile and yet was the quiet sustenance of my will to exist on my terms. Now that I'm in my midthirties, it has blossomed to a new expression. And if there is such a thing as reincarnation, I hope to continue returning as an intersex person.

Periods and Friendship

ANN FRIEDMAN
AND AMINATOU SOW

from: Ann Friedman
to: Aminatou Sow
date: Mon., Apr. 17, 2017, at 1:40 PM
subject: Friendship and Periods

You know how some period-tracker apps let you share the details of your menstrual cycle with your friends? My first thought upon seeing that for the first time was, "If you're not already talking about your period with your friends, how close can you be?" Really. I can't remember exactly how I discussed my period with friends when I was a teenager, but in my adult friendships—ours included!—periods are such a normal part of the ongoing conversation. I almost always know when my closest boos are bleeding.

Women have been doing this since ancient times. And, let'sbereal, most of us don't need a special, cordoned-off space of a period app to talk about this stuff. It's woven through the text threads and brief check-ins and deep conversations that make up our friendships. My friends know that my cycle runs short, more like twenty-one days than twenty-eight. My friends know that day two is my worst for cramping. My friends know that my vagina hates applicators (the goddess gave you fingers for a reason). I know that you know all of this stuff, because we talk about periods the way we talk about all of the other daily details of our lives.

from: Aminatou Sow
to: Ann Friedman
date: Tues., Apr. 25, 2017, at 3:05 AM
subject: Re: Friendship and Periods

You're so right, women *have* been doing this since forever.

I remember period talk being an early bonding tool for us when we were new friends. I got mine at what felt like a young age, when I was eleven. None of my other friends did until we were at the end of middle school. I don't ever remember discussing it with high school friends either.

In fact, the woman who ran the athletic department made us all sign a pledge that we would never miss any practices because of our periods. At the time, I was foolish enough to think that was badass, and now I realize how limiting that kind of thinking is.

There's something so liberating about not being ashamed that we bleed. It can also help with diagnosing serious problems. I'm so embarrassed that I was well into my twenties when I realized that it wasn't okay I was having my period for weeks on end or that my cramps were well above an eight on the pain scale. I thought I just had to play through the pain—thanks for nothing, Coach Murray!—and now I know better.

The only redeeming part of having bad periods when you're an adult woman is that your friends can afford to buy you top-notch snacks and wine. That always helps. You brought Swedish Fish into my life during such a trying time and now they always make me think of you. You also never make fun of me when I use my laptop as a heating pad. #computerus

FYI NONE OF THIS IS MEDICAL ADVICE LOL

It's also not lost on me that you and I are lucky to live in a country where having a period didn't hold us back from going to school and having access to education like it does for so many girls around the world. Just Google "menstrual hygiene management" and prepare to have your mind blown by how much work we still have to do to educate folks about taboos around hygiene and reproductive health.

Do you remember ever feeling ashamed of your period?

from: Ann Friedman
to: Aminatou Sow
date: Wed., Apr. 26, 2017, at 3:25 PM
subject: Re: Friendship and Periods

Ughhh, yes. Ashamed, confused, repulsed. A whole cocktail of bad feelings. My early periods (around age twelve to thirteen) were some of the most painful and heaviest of my life. I remember being in church with my family once—there are multiple levels of horror and discomfort to this story—and kneeling made my cramps unbearable. (This was before I'd figured out how many ibuprofen I needed to survive the first few days of my period.) I shuffled out of the pew and back to the bathroom and spent the rest of the service sitting on a toilet in the women's room. Afterward I told my mom I'd filled a whole pad with blood in less than an hour, and she didn't believe me. I mean, I was never really into Catholicism, so I can see why she thought it was an excuse at the time. But because I was still so sensitive about my period, and still figuring out what "normal" was for me, her disbelief really stuck with me. It made me feel like a freak.

Because my mom and I didn't really talk about periods in depth, I relied on my friends for information. More precisely, I relied on my friends' moms' copies of *Redbook*. (Which is also where I learned about blow jobs and the gender wage gap. That magazine did so much for those of us who grew up pre-Internet and with conservative moms!) I was definitely not given a copy of *Our Bodies, Ourselves* or anything like that. And while it wasn't like my teenage friends and I were going deep on the finer points of our menstrual cycles, they were my first confidantes for questions and problems.

And a strong YES to the power of menstruation convos among adult women! Especially after my friends started dealing with serious health problems related to their uteruses, or after they got IUDs put in and suffered some intense, seemingly never-ending periods. It is a special pleasure and privilege of friendship to know when your pals are menstruating and therefore feeling extra sensitive, or needing to stay home with a #computerus. It feels so good to see your bestie on the doorstep with some Trader

Joe's brownie bites. Honestly, if I never menstruated I would not fully understand why they come in those giant tubs.

Do you see any posi aspects to getting a period?

from: Aminatou Sow
to: Ann Friedman
date: Sat., Apr. 29, 2017, at 11:29 PM
subject: Re: Friendship and Periods

I suppose it's helped me understand my body better and has turned out to be a great bonding experience with other women . . . but my god, at what price?

I guess I just wish I could have the posi experiences without the bleeding.

While I do think that it's really important to talk about our periods (the stigma and shame are so real!) and not feel that we inconvenience the world when we're leaving huuuuge bloodstains all over office chairs, I really don't think there's anything special or wonderful about actually bleeding.

I'M **REALLY WEARY** OF WHATEVER IT IS THAT WE ARE CALLING **PERIOD FEMINISM** THESE DAYS BECAUSE IT CAN ACTUALLY BE **REALLY ALIENATING** FOR A LOT OF FOLKS.

It's just a part of my biology. I didn't choose it, it doesn't make me better than anyone, and honestly, at least for me, it's a significant source of physical pain. Also, we can't forget that not every person who identifies as a woman actually has a period and having a period isn't what makes you a woman. Menstruation stigma is 100 percent definitely rooted in misogyny but that doesn't mean it only affects women. It's so dumb and harmful to conflate biology with gender and then isolate our trans and nonbinary pals with this kind of exclusive vocabulary and rituals around menstruation.

I'm really weary of whatever it is that we are calling Period Feminism these days because it can actually be really alienating for a lot of folks. There's a delicate balance between not being ashamed of our own bodies and making others feel inadequate about some fake biological empowerment narratives. Does that make sense? Ugh, gender essentialism is such a drag.

BTW, my cramps were so bad yesterday, I cried on the train back from DC. Time to call the doctor again. I have an ultrasound scheduled for next week and I'm so nervous about it.

from: Ann Friedman
to: Aminatou Sow
date: Tues., May 2, 2017, at 9:39 AM
subject: Re: Friendship and Periods

Ugh, I'm so sorry to hear about your Amtrak cry. Public transit while menstruating is the worst. We need to invent some way of strapping a heating pad to your abdomen for crampy days when leaving the house is a necessity. Please tell me how the ultrasound goes.

Thank you for bringing up so-called Period Feminism! I also feel pretty annoyed that openly and not-shamefully discussing something that happens to a lot of women (but definitely not all women, as you pointed out) has somehow become its own brand of feminism. It's absurd, and I blame the media's bottomless hunger for trend pieces. I don't want to go back to the era of body-denial when all menstrual-product ads featured a stream of blue liquid being squirted onto a pad, but there is such a thing as placing too much political weight on a simple biological reality.

It's also frustrating on a personal level, because the public conversations you and I have about our periods aren't intentionally about making menstruation central to feminism. They are simply a result of us—two women who happen to menstruate—talking openly about our bodies and our lives. In some of my other personal conversations, when my friends say shit about periods being goddess moon-cycle energy or the "divine feminine" or whatever, I get very annoyed. (Maybe this is a California problem?) Because, again, can we strike a balance, please? I'm not ashamed of my period, but I also don't credit it as a source of my power. Do you know what I mean?

from: Aminatou Sow
to: Ann Friedman
date: Fri., May 5, 2017, at 7:46 PM
subject: Re: Friendship and Periods

YES! I know exactly what you mean. Also, if we're being perfectly honest, the real source of my power probably has to do with how many snacks I eat all the time.

God. I dream of the day we have tampon ads with real blood and chunks instead of that ridiculous blue liquid. Can you imagine? It's weird that we refuse to acknowledge how completely banal blood is for people with periods. Come to think of it, the only time you see blood used in connection with women's bodies is when those crazy conservatives want to shock people with their awful, bloody antiabortion "art." The idea is that we're supposed to be grossed out by these images. Grossed out enough that we forego a completely normal procedure that's less dangerous than having a colonoscopy or actually having a baby. Our friend Rebecca Traister wrote a great column about this for *New York* magazine, "The Big Secret of Abortion: Women Already Know How It Works." If you have a period, blood and guts and chunks come as no surprise. It's not gross. It's our dang bodies.

I had my ultrasound. It came back all good. I actually laughed because the medical term for when everything is all good with an ultrasound is "unremarkable."

Never been so happy not to be special! I know I've been whining a lot but our bodies are pretty awesome. A real feat of biomedical engineering I will never tire of nerding out about.

PS—I'm reading that book you recommended, *Taking Charge of Your Fertility*. There is so much I didn't know about my body. I'm thirty-two—how is this possible?

from: Ann Friedman
to: Aminatou Sow
date: Sun., May 7, 2017, at 11:57 AM
subject: Re: Friendship and Periods

Never thought I'd say this, but I'm so happy to hear your bod is unremarkable!

Speaking of what *should* be unremarkable . . . *Taking Charge of Your Fertility* has rocked my thirty-five-year-old world, too. I've been recommending it to all my friends for the exact reason you mentioned: How is it possible I spent my whole life believing that all non-blood vaginal discharge was the same? The book explains that the different consistencies and types of cervical fluid correspond to phases and hormones in your cycle. It's really made me realize that the cultural shame around periods actually extends to all things ovulation. In the intro to the updated edition of this book, the author, Toni Weschler, describes how the first edition referred to "cervical mucus," but they changed it to "cervical fluid" because even women found the first phrase too disgusting to engage with. As a word person, I was interested in her theory, though I'm not sure she's right. I think it's less about linguistics and more about deeply ingrained body shame.

WHAT IF WE GOT THE MESSAGE THAT ALL BODIES ARE DIFFERENT, AND THE MOST IMPORTANT THING IS TO LEARN ABOUT YOURS?

Of course the book was recommended to me by a friend, too. I can't help but wonder: What if we were all just given this book back when we first hit puberty? What if we got the message that all bodies are different, and the most important thing is to learn about *yours*? It's so important to know what is truly "unremarkable" for you, because there is no universal normal.

from: Aminatou Sow
to: Ann Friedman
date: Mon., May 8, 2017, at 12:20 AM
subject: Re: Friendship and Periods

I really wish I could go back in a time machine and give this book to our tween selves. It would have definitely saved baby Amina a lot of grief and shame. Learning your body and unlearning the misinformation and lies you believe about your body really is a full-time process. I wish I'd started that journey earlier in life but I'm also so grateful for later-in-life friendships that have facilitated that for me.

I've been so encouraged and amused every single time I've complained or compared myself to someone else and you've said to me, "Bodies are different, Amina," in that resigned voice of yours. It's so true, Ann. Thanks for making space in our friendship to talk about this stuff. It's probably saved my life in the long run.

Can't wait to see you in a few weeks and cycle together, LOL. I'll have whiskey and snacks waiting. xo

from: Ann Friedman
to: Aminatou Sow
date: Mon., May 8, 2017 at 8:17 AM
subject: Re: Friendship and Periods

I can't take credit for "bodies are different," which I first heard from a friend. But I'm so happy to pass it along. And even happier to share this space of friendship with you. <3 I'm counting the days till our cycles (and snacks) sync up. . . .

Going with the Flow:

Blood and Sisterhood at the London Marathon

A MODERN PERIOD PIECE BY

MADAME GANDHI

Originally written April 2015, Revised July 2017

"It's a radical notion realizing that on a
marathon course you don't have to worry
about how you look for others."

Have you ever run a marathon on day one of your period?

MILE 1

I got my flow the night before the London Marathon and it was extremely painful. It would be my first marathon and I remember already feeling so nervous for it. I had spent a full year enthusiastically training hard, yet I had never actually practiced running on my period.

I thought through my options. Running 26.2 miles with a wad of cotton material wedged between my legs just seemed so absurd. Plus they say chafing is a real thing. I honestly didn't know what to do. I knew that I was lucky to have access to menstrual products, to be part of a society that at least has a "norm" built around periods. I definitely had the choice to participate in this norm at the expense of my own comfort and just deal with it quietly.

But then I thought . . . if there's one person society can't shame, it's a marathon runner. You can't tell a marathoner to adhere to problematic social norms, asking them to prioritize the comfort of others at the expense of their own, as women long have. On the marathon course, I could choose whether or not I wanted to participate in the oppressive social norm of period shaming.

So I decided to reject the stigma surrounding women's cycles, take some Midol for the pain, bleed freely, and just run.

A marathon is a centuries-old symbolic act. Why not leverage this experience to draw light to those who don't have access to menstrual care products? Or to those who, despite their cramping and pain, have to hide it away and pretend like it doesn't exist?

MILE 6

I ran the marathon with two women who were very close to me, Ana and Mere. Both of them had done marathons before. I assumed we would definitely end up splitting up during the run, but by mile six they were still with me, right at my side. Their generosity to support my run was so deeply inspiring. It made me want to keep going for them.

SO I DECIDED TO REJECT THE STIGMA SURROUNDING WOMEN'S CYCLES, TAKE SOME MIDOL FOR THE PAIN, BLEED FREELY, AND JUST RUN.

As I ran, I thought about how all of us have been effectively socialized to pretend periods don't exist. By establishing an expectation of period shaming, many modern societies prevent the opportunity to actually bond over an experience that half of the world's population will likely have in their life. An experience that could bring women and people who menstruate even closer. An experience that enables the cycle of life! With such a taboo surrounding periods, we don't have the language to freely express pain in the workplace, and we don't acknowledge the experience of bleeding bodies. Because it is all kept quiet, we are socialized not to complain or talk about essential bodily functions. No one can see it happening. And if you can't see it, it's probably "not a big deal." But this is an important issue. Stigma is one of the most effective forms of oppression because it denies us the ability to speak comfortably and confidently about our own bodies. It reiterates the notion that women are only valued for their looks and sexual attractiveness to men. And so, in an effort to use shock culture to force society to question one of its most oppressive norms, I started bleeding freely.

MILE 7

I was going through all these crazy thoughts and analyzing whether I was either:

a) A crazy chick who needed to just calm down and reach for a tampon
(Someone came up behind me, making a disgusted face, to tell me in a subdued voice that I was on my period. . . . Wow, I had NO idea!)

Or

b) A liberated boss madame who loved her own body, was running an effing marathon, and was not in the mood for being oppressed that day

MILE 8

As we came up on mile eight, I saw my dad and brother. They were so completely amazing—smiling and laughing and cheering. I kept trying to awkwardly pull my shirt down to my knees so they wouldn't see that I was bleeding. But as I approached them, I realized they just wanted to scream and hug and take a photo and celebrate together. They were so in the moment with me and there was so much love. The two most important men in my life couldn't have cared less about blood.

Ana's mom and sister were both there, too, screaming and holding up adorable signs all throughout the race—seeing them made us feel uplifted, like part of something epic.

MILE 13.1

Around us we saw other people engaged in pain and persecution—running barefoot, running while singing karaoke, running with a forty-pound backpack, and one guy even running as Jesus with a huge wooden cross on his back! Everyone running was on their own personal mission. And all of a sudden, it felt like it was meant to be that I got my period on marathon day.

The sidelines were packed, and maybe it was delirium and exhaustion, but every single sign I read was hilarious. Even the hydration signs. I was in love with them.

MILE 18.5

They say you hit a wall at 18.5 miles, so I tried to focus on my next milestone. The first was to get to mile six, then to mile eight to see family, then the half marathon point at 13.1 over the bridge, then to mile 18.5 to see the breast cancer cheer point (we ran for Breast Cancer Care), and then the final stretch to 26.2.

AS I RAN, I THOUGHT ABOUT HOW ALL OF US HAVE BEEN EFFECTIVELY SOCIALIZED TO **PRETEND PERIODS DON'T EXIST**.

I remember thinking, *My body has my back so hard right now. The female body is incredible. We haven't even stopped running once. I want us to finish strong*. We didn't stop running once.

FINISH LINE

The 2015 London Marathon was everything for me. I trained for a year and then it happened and it really was an incredible, unforgettable thing. We ran for women who can't show their periods in public and for women who can't compete in athletic events. We ran for our friends who have suffered through period cramps while doing work, and for women who have survived breast cancer. We ran for those who are afraid to bleed because of their gender identity. We ran in solidarity side by side and we crossed the finish line hand in hand.

To this day, I analyze a lot of what I do against how I felt during the marathon. I recall the strength to channel positivity and to value working as a team over working individually. I think about goal-setting and executing. I think about pain and fear, and what it feels like to overcome them. And I think about feminism, body positivity, and having the ovaries to practice what you preach.

I Can't Walk but I Can Bleed

SANTINA MUHA

I want to start by saying that while I may be in a wheelchair, I'm only definitively speaking for myself here. I can tell you how I do things. Just like people who can walk all handle their periods differently, all have different preferences and symptoms and flows, so do people who can't walk. For example, I have full use of my arms and hands, and am considered very high functioning. I live alone, shower on my own, get myself dressed, etc. People with higher levels of injury than me, such as quadriplegics, often need assistance with daily routines, and so they may need more assistance when they're menstruating. So while I can make some assumptions about what it's like to have your period as a girl in a wheelchair, I never want to seem like I'm speaking on everyone's behalf in any way. But, since I'm here, I may as well tell you a little bit about how I deal with my period in my situation.

A car accident when I was almost six years old severed my spine at the T-11 level, which means I am paralyzed at the eleventh vertebrae of the thoracic level, or more simply, from the waist down. In elementary school, this never really seemed to matter. Actually, it kind of made me cool because young kids love riding things with wheels. I rode to school in my own special bus and I got to skip gym whenever I wanted. And because my insurance company had to make my house compliant with the ADA (Americans with Disabilities Act), my bedroom and personal bathroom were *huge*, bigger than my parents'. Yes, that's right, I had my own personal bathroom at the age of seven. I felt a little bit like a celebrity.

Kids would ask me dumb questions, because they were kids, and I'd be excited to answer them because I felt like I was smart and experienced. Questions like: "How do you sleep if you're in a wheelchair?" And I'd say, "Well, I transfer into my bed and lie down and sleep, just like you! Want to see?" And then I'd show them how I transfer and I was seriously the coolest.

But then came middle school, which was a weird time for me because that's when kids start to want to blend in. I was a young girl just trying to be like everyone else, yet I was the only girl in my school in a wheelchair. Pretty ironic how the girl in the wheelchair can't help but stand out, huh?

Being in a wheelchair in middle school still drew a lot of attention from kids, but not the cool attention I was used to. Now they were asking me questions I didn't know the answers to yet, like: "Can you have sex?" How was I supposed to know? I was twelve! I didn't know what was working down there or how. I had had several surgeries on my stomach area and even my bladder, but as far as I knew, my ovaries and all that were in normal shape. I mean, there was no chapter in fifth-grade health class about paralyzed girls, so I just assumed everything they were teaching the class applied to me.

No one had ever taken me aside, no doctor had ever mentioned it to me, and my mom had never given me any warnings that I might be different. So when my friends started getting their periods, I got excited because I knew mine must be coming soon. And I knew that would make me just like my friends again. Well, at least in one category of life for one week of every month.

I remember one weekend when I was in sixth grade, my BFFJES (Best Friend For Just Elementary School) was sleeping over and she got her period and my mom had to get her a clean pair of pants to wear. I was so jealous. At pool parties that summer a few girls would say they couldn't go swimming because they were on their periods. They whispered it and pretended to be embarrassed about it, but you could totally tell they were secretly bragging.

I still hadn't gotten mine yet, but I was holding strong. I wasn't afraid. I honestly can't remember a time when I thought being paralyzed would affect whether or not I'd get my period. Also, it's worth it to note that back then I was less afraid of everything. Not only did I never think being in a wheelchair would affect my dating life, but I thought I would actually marry Luke Perry (aka in my day Dylan McKay on *Beverly Hills, 90210*; currently aka Archie's dad on *Riverdale*). If periods were a thing we didn't get until we were in our twenties, I probably would have started worrying about it every day starting on my twentieth birthday. Because now I worry about everything! But then I didn't.

And then, one day, one glorious day that I can't remember at all but it must have happened because I totally have my period, I got my period! I seriously cannot remember a thing about it. I didn't celebrate or have a period party. My mom didn't buy me a "becoming a woman" gift. I always used to ask my mom how old she was when she got her period and she'd say, "I don't remember—thirteen? Fourteen?" I couldn't believe she couldn't remember this monumental moment of her life. And now, if you ask me how old I was when I got my period, I say the same exact thing. It had to be sometime around that age, though, because in seventh grade my boobs were an A cup, and in eighth grade they were suddenly a C cup. I also got my braces off and started wearing makeup then. It was a real *She's All That* year for me. I'm sure I secretly bragged every chance I got for the next few months so the world would know I was officially a woman (which is delusional because now, almost twenty years later, I still don't know if I'm officially a "woman"). But at the time I thought that was it. It was official.

Of course at the time I was a teenager, and I was one of those terrible teenage girls who are so happy and fun around their friends, but so exasperated and humiliated and angry around their mother and close family members. I'd say I wasn't bad enough for my mom to take me on the terrible teens episodes of *The Maury Show*, but I was bad enough for her to make me watch those episodes when I got home from school. So since I was already angsty and sad and angry every other minute, I wasn't too mad about having PMS. If anything, I liked it for giving me an excuse for being a little bitchy at least twelve weeks of the year.

It wasn't until my teenage brain started to mellow out a little that I could feel the contrast of emotions during that special time of the month. I started to hate PMS. And this is where being paralyzed comes back into play.

Our bodies do this amazing thing where they send us signals when we're in pain. But there are certain areas of my body that I can't feel as well as others. Don't think this gets me out of cramps. If I'm experiencing menstrual pain in a part of my body that I can't "feel," my body will sort of redirect the pain to a place where I can feel. A more technical term for this is autonomic dysreflexia. Autonomic dysreflexia typically affects people with a slightly higher level of injury than I have (more like T-6), but I have experienced some symptoms. For example, when I was younger, I fractured my femur. I couldn't feel the pain in my leg, so I didn't know I had injured myself, but then I started experiencing chills, a fever, a terrible headache, and blurry vision. These same things occur when I have a urinary tract infection. And when I'm having a particularly bad month in the menstruation department, these same symptoms can pop up then.

If you think about it, you can imagine how confusing and frustrating this might be. Whenever I get a very bad headache, not only do I have to ask myself if I drank enough water today or am I stressed out or any of the usual suspects that cause a headache, I also have to inspect my body to make sure there are no obvious breaks or bruises or issues below the belt. What this means for my period is that most months I have the pleasure of feeling cramps in the parts where I can feel, then a migraine from the parts that I can't feel as much. Cool, right? :-/ I mean, I guess it really is cool and amazing that our bodies do that, but also I wouldn't mind catching a break and not feeling the pain at all!

When my body is going crazy, feeling pain and sending it to different places, my brain gets confused and then I get agitated and that's when all the worst stuff starts happening. Like that feeling where if you killed someone, you think you could probably get off on insanity because your brain doesn't even feel like itself in that moment (I'm exaggerating—please don't think I'm a killer, but you know what I mean).

Sometimes I used to get so mad and I'd know it was too mad. I could still hear that rational part in my brain that's like, "Um, I think we're overreacting right now." But my period brain is strong. She's like, "WHAT?? YOU THINK WE'RE OVERREACTING? OH REALLY? SO SOMEONE TAKES THE LAST STRING CHEESE THAT YOU THOUGHT YOU WERE

GOING TO EAT (or insert dumb thing to be mad about here) AND YOU JUST WANT US TO MOVE ON AND NOT LET THEM KNOW HOW THIS MADE YOU FEEL?!?! HOW WILL THEY EVER LEARN? ARE YOU A PUSHOVER? DO I LIVE IN A PUSHOVER'S HEAD? I DON'T THINK SO." And then my rational brain is like, "Okay, okay, you win. Go nuts."

Period brain intimidates rational brain every time. I got on birth control way before I started having sex for this reason. My gyno said it could help with symptoms. I don't know if it did. I have no idea. But I'm still on birth control to this day, mostly because I'm afraid if I go off of it I'll experience terrible hormonal symptoms and that terrifies me. On the flip side, though, birth control can increase your chances of forming blood clots, which I'm already at risk for in my situation, so I'm starting to explore my options in regards to this.

Then there are the things I have to think about when it comes to my method of stopping the blood flow. When I was younger, I used tampons much more than I do now. I learned how to use tampons like many girls do, I think—from a friend. In my case from my best friend, Cindy, who was one year older than me. Cindy was on the other side of my personal bathroom door, giving me verbal instructions in real time. It took a few tries, but I finally got it. My other best friend, Jen, who was a year younger than me, recently reminded me that I was the one who taught her how to put in a tampon over the phone, so I guess that proves my theory. Also, neither Cindy nor Jen are paralyzed, so that goes to show putting in a tampon is pretty universal. It's interesting that I made Cindy stand on the other side of the door, because she'd been in the bathroom with me hundreds of times when I peed. But for some reason, this was a more private—maybe even sacred—event. To this day, when a friend and I go into a restroom as a pair, I don't think twice about them being there while I'm peeing, but when I have my period I ask them to turn around. I know as a fellow ovary carrier they've seen period blood. And I don't know why my brain makes it more gross than pee. I guess because it's messier? Either way, I usually warn them it looks like a zombie movie down there and could they please just face the door for a minute? As I was writing that, I was thinking, "Is that TMI?" but then I realized everything I'm telling you is TMI and that's why you're reading!

So let me explain why I'm more of a pad girl now. Neither are comfortable. But tampons scare me. I try to stay away from illnesses that give you confusing symptoms, since I already have enough of that going on, and that's exactly what toxic shock syndrome (TSS) sounds like it does. I know TSS is very rare, but it is associated with tampon use, and I don't want to risk it even if it's never going to happen. I already have to be very careful, as someone living with a spinal cord injury, to pay attention to my body and look out for signals of autonomic dysreflexia. I don't want to increase my chances of anything else, because I may not recognize the symptoms and just chalk it up to my body reacting to my period, sending signals everywhere. Although now that I've Googled it and I know I can get TSS from bacteria getting in my bloodstream even if I'm not wearing a tampon, I'm probably going to be scared I have it all the time.

So I basically just stick to pads. (No pun intended. Just kidding—pun always intended.) I'm sitting most of the time anyway, so I don't have to worry too much about my butt looking bulky. Also, and I guess this is one of the advantages to being in a wheelchair when you get your period, if there's any accidental bleed through, you can't really see it because you can't see my behind area. (Which usually I'm mad about. Thank God I have big boobs to make up for it. I may not be pulling in any butt guys, but I got those boob guys on lock.) Also, while we're on the subject of bleeding through, here's a pro tip in case you didn't know it—hydrogen peroxide gets out bloodstains really well.

So I guess having my period is mostly the same for me as it is for someone who isn't paralyzed. One instance where I wish I could walk is when I'm not expecting to get it and I sit on the toilet to pee and realize, oops, I got my period. I can't get up and run to my room and grab a clean pair of underwear. But I just need to plan ahead a little. I try to always keep a clean pair of underwear in one of the drawers next to my toilet, along with pads, baby wipes, and a towel. Being in a wheelchair calls for a lot of thinking ahead. And because I always carry a "just in case" bag on my wheelchair, I always have pads and tampons on me. And hair ties. And gummy candy. Okay, I'm a rolling CVS.

I HAVE NO PROBLEM TELLING A ROOM FULL OF PEOPLE, MALE AND/OR FEMALE, THAT I'M ON MY PERIOD. IT'S A PART OF LIFE. IT'S LITERALLY A PART OF THE CREATION OF LIFE.

Sometimes we think of periods as a humiliating thing. But we shouldn't. I mean, was I embarrassed that Christmas when my dog dragged my bloody pads out of the garbage and into the living room for all to see? Of course. And thank you to my mom for cleaning that situation up as quickly as she could. But about half the population gets their period. I have no problem telling a room full of people, male and/or female, that I'm on my period. It's a part of life. It's literally a part of the creation of life. It's not an easy thing to deal with every single month. But as much as I complain about my period when I have it, I guess there's a part of me that likes it, or at least appreciates it. There are too many conversations I don't feel like I can fully participate in with my girlfriends already, such as how bad their feet feel after a day of walking around in heels, or how hard it is to hover over a public toilet, or how they don't feel like getting something because it's all the way upstairs. But I *can* trade stories with my girlfriends about heavy flows and PMS-y moments. I can cancel a thing I didn't really want to do anyway because my cramps are too much, just like they do. I can be late and wonder if somehow, someway, even though we did everything right, I could be pregnant. So yes, in many ways I'm different. But for better or worse, I can complain about my period with the best of them. And I think that's pretty great.

There's a First for Everything

INGRID NILSEN

Experiencing a first in life is always memorable—whether it's your first day of school, first kiss, or first loss of a loved one. Firsts are often signifiers of one door closing and another door opening. They are powerful new beginnings that will shape us in ways that are only revealed to us through the grace of time. So, as someone who has now been menstruating for almost fifteen years, I'm able to look back on some of my period firsts in ways I never have before. My period, as annoying, frustrating, and painful as it can be sometimes, has taught me so much about my body and my life. Here are three pivotal, bloody moments.

MY FIRST TIME

At fifteen, I was the last person in my circle of friends to get her period. I had been faking it for about a year, not wanting to be left out of the "What do you use?" and "Ugh, cramps suck!" conversations. These seemingly small, mundane interactions were ultimately moments of sincere bonding among girls around me; something I noticed and felt excluded from. So every day, I wished and prayed that I would receive the keys to this ultra-elite kingdom. I thought the day would never come—until it finally did.

Menarche came for me on a Saturday. I woke up thirsty, so I went downstairs in a sleepy daze and poured myself a glass of orange juice. My underwear felt kind of wet, which was a little weird, but I brushed it off as standard vaginal discharge. I had been so vigilant and on "period watch" for so long— there was no way *this* was *that* moment.

I had every intention of getting back into bed but went to the bathroom for a quick pee. It was early in the morning and the sun was just coming up over the trees in our backyard. I was on autopilot, just trying to find the fastest route back to sleep. My eyes were heavy, and as I sat on the toilet, I looked around the room to keep myself from nodding off. To my left, I saw the new plastic shower curtain my mom had just put up. The pattern was a slightly different variation of the same thing we always had in that bathroom: fish. Directly in front of me was the towel rack. I could see the little chips in the paint that were only visible when the rack was bare. They were literal pieces from my past, probably going back to when I was about six or seven and insisted on putting stickers everywhere, despite my parents telling me not to.

Then I looked down. I jumped. I was so startled when I saw my baby-blue Paul Frank pajamas covered in blood. They were soaked. I couldn't even see the original color of my underwear. Everything was covered in crimson goop. I went to wipe myself, and there was even more blood on the tissue. I thought I was going to pass out, but instead I burst into tears and got into bed with my mom—bloody pj's and all.

I WAS EXPECTING MAYBE A COUPLE DIME-SIZE SPOTS OF BLOOD, NOT WHAT LOOKED LIKE A MASSACRE IN MY PANTS!

In my brain, I knew what was happening. I knew this was my period. I had seen those weird, outdated videos in school and even had a body book that I had secretly ordered from the book order in elementary school. Plus, every girl I knew had her period. But when it happened to me, it was a shock to my system. Nobody told me it would be like *this*. I was expecting maybe a couple dime-size spots of blood, not what looked like a massacre in my pants! It was gooey and mucusy, not at all like the blood you see when you cut yourself. I was so confused. Was this normal? Was something wrong with me? I just kept sobbing to my mom. I remember her immediately sitting up in bed with concern all over her face, but relaxing and smiling with relief when I said I had gotten my period.

This is actually one of the fondest memories I have in my Mom Memory Bank. We weren't particularly close, especially in my teen years, but I remember how gentle she was with me that day. How she calmed and soothed me, telling me that all of this was totally normal and that I'd be okay. She gave me a pad to hold me over while we went shopping so I could pick out my own pads and get some dark underwear. For the first time as a teenager, my mom helped me feel okay with my body and the things it was doing. As it turned out, my period didn't exactly give me the keys to the kingdom of cool, but it did give me the keys to something I wanted on a deeper level: connection and a moment of bonding with my mom, someone

I had always felt distant from. So I guess I got my wish—it just looked a little different than I had expected. Kind of like my period.

DIRTY GIRL

I started to free myself from period shame in 2010. Admittedly, I was probably more comfortable with my period than anyone else I knew, but there was this one thing that was really holding me back: pads. If you're a menstruating human, you've probably overheard or participated in conversations about how "gross" pads are at some point in your life. Even as a pad user myself, I can definitely check both of those boxes.

I'm not exactly sure where all this pad shaming started, but I'd guess cis men had something to do with it. I've seen and heard what many men think of periods in general and pads more specifically—men who aren't necessarily bad people. They think periods are gross. They think tampons are "less dirty" and more sanitary because they're inside your body and less noticeable. They get uncomfortable if their girlfriend is wearing a pad because it feels like she's wearing a diaper. The list goes on and on. So naturally, this makes women feel awful and ashamed of their bodies and their choices. We internalize this and try to find ways to be less "gross" and more appealing. Pad shaming, unfortunately, is one of those solutions.

Now, I'm not here to go into some long analysis about our cultural and social views on menstruation (even though it's one of my favorite topics), but I wanted to give a nugget of context before getting into the main event: the two people who helped me free myself from pad shame, one of whom is . . . Surprise! A man.

I.

I was living in San Francisco in 2010 with a few roommates in a loft apartment. I shared a tiny room downstairs with one girl. Despite the cramped quarters, it was a dream rooming with her. We shared a bathroom, a mutual level of respect, and a love for MAC makeup, and agreed from day one to be communicative and open when it came to our space. On top of that, she was hilarious and incredibly kind. When someone talked, she listened, and not in the way of just nodding her head and then proceeding to talk about herself. I mean *really* listened. The kind of listening where someone doesn't say anything, but they look you in the eyes and they see you, and that's enough.

Needless to say, I loved living together, but there was one moment when I really felt like I put our relationship on the line. You see, sometimes when I take a shower and I'm on my period, I just take off my underwear and leave my pad still in it. This is because: (a) I'm lazy, and (b) I wrap my used pad in a new pad's wrapper, and I'm not going to be putting on a new pad until I'm out of the shower. Logistically it just doesn't make sense to dispose of the old one until I'm done. So bloody-pad underwear on the floor it is!

Usually, this is a seamless process. No one knows any of this is happening. Except this one time when I showered while on my period, and my roommate needed to use the bathroom. I was so focused on getting out quickly so she could get in that I ran out in my towel and completely forgot to grab my underwear. Now you may be thinking that I had it off in a corner, somewhere not so noticeable, but NOPE! It was smack-dab in the middle of the floor *and* it wasn't a light day, so there was blood all over that thing. I realized this as soon as she was in and shut the door. I paced outside, waiting for her to scream in disgust, but there was nothing. Maybe she was so grossed out that she had been shocked into silence? To say I was mortified would be an understatement.

A couple of minutes (which seemed like hours) passed and she came out of the bathroom. I anxiously looked at her with apologetic eyes, waiting for her to say something. She looked at me, totally confused. I immediately started apologizing and trying to explain myself and she stopped me in the middle of my rambling. She said, "It's okay. It's no big deal. It doesn't bother me at all." I was shocked. Dumbfounded. She meant it, too. She proceeded to go on with her day, completely unfazed.

As I went into the bathroom and picked

up my underwear, I remember thinking that this was a moment to remember. I didn't know why, but I felt like it was significant deep down inside me, and I was right. I was harboring shame over wearing pads and my little bathroom habit. To have someone see all of those things, plus what my actual menstrual blood looked like (which no one had seen except myself), and not bat an eye or see me differently—that was huge. My roommate made me see myself and my body in a different light: a body filled with a heart and mind and soul that was worthy of friendship and love. That day, when I threw out the used pad that I'd left on the bathroom floor, I threw out all the years of shame that came with it.

II. GOING THE DISTANCE

Interestingly, a few weeks after the pad-on-the-floor incident, I found myself in another predicament: getting my period while I was with the guy I was dating at the time and being totally unprepared for it. This had never happened to me before.

We were in his apartment chatting; he was sitting at his desk and I was standing at the foot of his bed. Usually my period starts with a few light drops and I have about an hour before full flow is in effect. This was not one of those times. As I stood in his room, I felt a rush of wetness in my crotch. And not the "Ooooh, I'm into this!" kind of wetness. It was my period and it was here in full force.

I froze. My eyes probably looked like I had seen a ghost and I could feel my heart racing. In the past, the guys I had dated wanted nothing to do with my period. I was newly dating this guy, so I really had no idea where he stood with it all, but based off previous experiences I was guessing he'd probably fall into the same boat. I was wrong. Oh so very wrong. When he saw me freeze, he immediately asked what was wrong. I blurted out, "My period just started." I felt trapped. I could only move as far as the bathroom to stuff tissues down my pants because every movement I made just prompted more blood to come out. I knew this was a temporary solution and so did he. He calmly asked me, "What do you need?" and I said, "Pads."

He proceeded to run out the door, out of the building, around the corner, and down the street to the nearest convenience store. I know this because I was standing by the window and saw him bolting down the sidewalk. I had never seen anyone move so fast for me. I smiled, and in that moment I knew he was special. I knew this moment was special. I hadn't had the best relationship experience prior to this. I had been hurt. I had hurt people. I had been taken advantage of. I had been raped. And I had definitely never had a boyfriend who would go out and buy me pads. When he returned, he was out of breath but smiled as he gave me the plastic bag containing my pads. I was so relieved.

Over the course of our relationship together, relief was a common theme. He brought down my walls and he was living proof that kindness, acceptance, a willingness to learn, and a capacity for compassion can exist in all men. Eventually our relationship ended because we were moving to different cities, but I've never forgotten our time together. He was the first man I had been romantically involved with who truly accepted me. He was my first lesson in finding the people who will go the distance for you.

DOING THE WORK

As I sit here now, almost eight years later, I see how much my life has changed. I have a job that allows me to express my creativity and put meaningful work out into the world. I have a small group of best friends that I'd do anything for. I've come out as lesbian and I'm dating a badass woman I absolutely adore. Plus, my mom and I are closer than ever. I've experienced a lot more period firsts, too: trying menstrual cups and discs, having sex on my period, and publicly asking President Obama about the luxury tax on menstrual products (he had no idea it even existed!). Through all these moments and seasons of life, I have worked hard, kept faith, and continued to menstruate. My period has helped me examine the world through a different lens. I see the beauty, the history, the science, and the inequality that permeates our social interactions and government. All of this just because 50 percent of the population is shedding some uterine lining. I don't think anyone who has a period would consider this totally natural bodily function a luxury. So why are we treated like we're lesser than, while simultaneously being charged more for our biology? Why is reform being pitched to and then denied by panels of cis men who have never had a period in their lives? When will they get over themselves, step aside, and listen?

Yeah, this is all pretty daunting, but despite the seemingly impossible obstacles, change is happening if you look closely. Our voices are growing and getting louder. History knows we make the impossible a reality. We're in this battle and we're out here for blood.

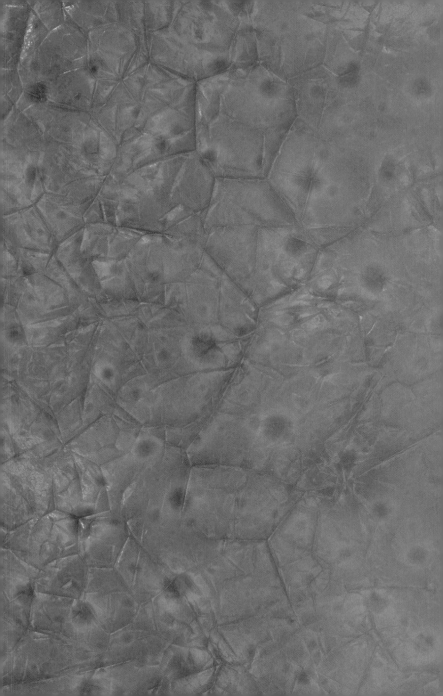

My Period and Me:
A Trans Guy's Guide
to Menstruation

WILEY READING

I'm doing the cramp wiggle at my desk chair
right now.

You know, the seat acrobatics you do
when you've got cramps, but you're too lazy
to get up and get Advil, and it hasn't gotten
bad enough yet that you've got to lie on the
ground with your butt up in the air.

It's funny. When I initially began writing this, I hadn't had anything resembling a period in months. And then my doctor switched my birth control on me, and my reproductive organs took full advantage of the slight change in hormones. My body really, really wants to menstruate, y'all.

Oh. This might be a good time to mention that I'm a dude—one with a uterus. A very, very excitable uterus.

I actually did okay when the Great Body Part Mechanic in the Sky was handing out body parts. I have broad shoulders; fat settles on my belly instead of my thighs; and I have narrow hips. I'm built like a little bull (or refrigerator).

So although I don't take testosterone, my body looks male in many ways that are important to me.

Unfortunately, there's still my reproductive system.

When I got my period—at eleven—I discovered that my female hormones were just about as excited about menstruation as they could possibly be.

I used to think that this was something I'd just have to deal with, like my small hands and long eyelashes. But then my psychiatrist prescribed me birth control pills.

She had correctly identified that I'm least emotionally stable in the weeks before and after my period. So I got to take birth control for "continuous suppression of periods."

I mostly get to forget that I can have periods. But I can't pretend that I'm going to be able to avoid it permanently. Every once in a while, I have a full-blown period attack.

So that's my life. My period is going to period whenever it gets the chance.

It's not easy. Everyone in the world thinks periods are the ultimate expression of femininity. Sometimes it makes me feel very, very feminine.

But the truth is, there's no reason bleeding makes me feminine. Gynecomastia doesn't make men women, and my period doesn't make me one either.

Most trans guys have to deal with their periods at some point or another. It's not something we talk about—a lot of us are ashamed, which is understandable.

But this shouldn't be a shameful thing. We should be able to talk about what our bodies are doing and help one another out with tips and support.

I'm trying to start a conversation both about why menstruation isn't an inherently female thing—if trans men experience it, it can't be truly female, can it?—and how talking about our bodies is sometimes the best way to fight gender dysphoria and learn new things about how to improve our lives.

Periods happen to lots and lots of people. Many of them are women and girls, but those of us who are something else should have a context for our experience and a way of talking about it without being misgendered.

So here's what I do to help myself feel better when I'm getting a visit from Aunt Period.

I. AVOID "FEMININE PRODUCTS"

I like to not wear pads or tampons or any sort of quote-unquote "feminine product."

This is not possible for everyone, and it's not even possible for me without the aid of birth control.

When I do need to buy them, sometimes I ask my girlfriend to buy them for me; sometimes I make a lot of jokes about it in my head. I remind myself that the cashier definitely does not care what I'm purchasing. If I'm feeling particularly fragile about it, I avoid stores where I might run into the same cashier again.

But when it is possible, it makes me feel more like myself experiencing a medical condition and less like I'm a lady flower experiencing lady uterus ladyship.

2. TREAT IT WITH A SENSE OF HUMOR

For example, I call it a "man period." I joke to myself about it. I joke to my friends and girlfriend about it.

I make it silly so it's less likely to upset me. If I make light of it, it has less power over me.

Silly things don't cause deep emotions.

When you trip over your shoelaces in front of your mean-girl coworkers, you can make it serious: Wonderful, now they're gonna think I'm klutzy; or you can make it funny: Of course I had to trip just then. Perhaps I should take up ballet.

It's not easy to embrace the latter perspective, but I've found when you make yourself take things less seriously, everyone else follows suit.

3. REMEMBER THAT ANATOMY ISN'T A BINARY

It helps to remind myself that there are more similarities between "male" and "female" anatomy than there are differences.

I'm not going to get ejected from the realm of masculinity because my set of gonads produces blood from time to time. I didn't get "born into the wrong body." I just developed a little differently from some guys.

We all have the same basic stuff. My junk just got a little confused along the way.

Also, we have this idea that there are male genitals and female genitals and nothing in between, and that they are polar opposites. This couldn't be further from the truth.

Human sexuality is a glorious mess, and it makes me feel better to know that I'm not at the wrong end of the binary. I'm just somewhere on the spectrum like everyone else.

4. TALK TO OTHER TRANS GUYS ABOUT IT

A lot of trans guys have periods, for whatever reason. And a lot of them are very philosophical about it. I definitely recommend talking to them.

I find it's easier to put things in perspective when I feel like I'm not the only one experiencing something.

I have some male friends who still get their periods, and they experience a range of feelings about it, but hearing a trans guy complain about getting his period like it's a totally normal thing for a dude to complain about makes me feel like I can treat it like a totally normal thing to complain about, too.

MY BODY IS **NOT FEMALE**. MY MENSTRUATION IS NOT FEMALE. IT JUST *IS*. MY BODY JUST IS.

Talking about your reproductive organs as a masculine-identified person is a political act. If we openly talk about it, there's less shame. If there's less shame, there's less pain and more acceptance.

5. LET GO OF EXPECTATIONS

Lastly, and most simply, I try to let go of my expectations.

We all grow up with a link between sex and gender and ideas about what's intrinsically male and female.

Even though I have more information now, and I know intellectually that sex and gender aren't as simple as I was raised to believe, it takes time to override my upbringing.

I may have to remind myself over and over again that having a period doesn't make me female any more than having nipples makes someone a mother, but someday I'll overcome my conditioned ideas of sex and gender and be able to fully accept that men can have periods.

My body is not female. My menstruation is not female. It just *is*. My body just is.

My body is its own thing. It does what it

does, and that's fine. Getting my period is painful and bloody and messy and annoying, but it doesn't have to make me feel like less of a guy.

The amount of pain I hear from trans men related to their periods is substantial. But by talking about it and degendering it, we can lessen the pain.

Menstruating doesn't have to be a girl thing.

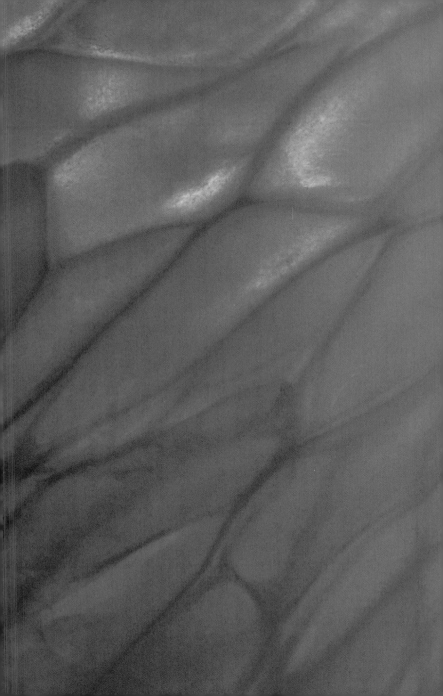

Black Blood

ASHLEY REESE

In the rare moments when pop culture stops clutching its pearls for two seconds and acknowledges that periods are an actual thing instead of a tablespoon of blue liquid on a maxi pad, television, movies, and books always depict a first period in such a grandiose manner. There's the overenthusiastic mother who considers first periods revelatory and calls for a celebration of the menses persuasion. Or there's the scenario where a character's first period starts in front of their crush, leading to mortification of the highest level. And then you have something like *Carrie*, in which periods are couched in this kind of body horror that, if anything, is a lot more realistic than Mom baking a "Congrats on getting your period" cake.

I don't have an endearing first-period story.

Look, I don't know about *your* family, but *mine* wasn't about to throw me a party commemorating the day that I started bleeding out of my vagina. God, the thought of my dad even knowing what a period was or that his only child had one made me want to die as a kid, and it low-key still does now. As far as I'm concerned, puberty never happened and I'm okay with keeping it that way, thank you very much.

Instead, my recollections of my first period go a little something like this: I woke up one summer morning, noticed a ruddy-brown substance in my underwear, and immediately went into full denial mode. I spent the entire day in disbelief. I tried to make a convincing case to my mom about how I didn't, in fact, just start my period. It was all a fluke, some weird mistake, some pre-period period to keep my guard up. My mom gave me a panty liner just in case, but even then I could hear the skepticism in her voice when she pretended to agree with me. We met up with a friend and her mom to see a soon-to-be-forgotten PG-13 comedy—*Rat Race*—we ate chili cheese fries afterward, and by the end of the day, I'd accepted the truth. I'd started my period, and it was terrible. I spent the rest of that weekend watching *Anne of Green Gables* on PBS and smothering all of my food in garlic salt.

I was ten years old, going on eleven, and I felt too young to suddenly have to grow up, to be responsible for my body's maintenance like a mechanic, to head down the path of adulthood, whatever the hell that was. I was a child, the youngest in my class. I just wasn't ready.

Shortly after that, 9/11 happened.

Abrupt, I know, but whenever I think about my first period, my memories flesh themselves out as follows: underwear horror show, the movie, the plush red leatherette seats of the restaurant where I ate the chili cheese fries, PBS, and September fucking 11. It's like the quintessential grim millennial coming-of-age story. I went from discovering what it was like to menstruate to learning what a terrorist was within the course of a couple of weeks. From ignorant bodily bliss, to rude awakening, to acceptance, to witnessing the most important geopolitical event in generations and realizing that life was more than *Lizzie McGuire* reruns.

Again, I was ten years old.

This might come across as a trite comparison, but I really do view these two moments in a combo deal of formative hell. I had anxiety about the world at large and about the rush of blood that would exit my body on a monthly basis, and I felt entirely too young to cope. It wasn't until I was older that I realized that I really *was* a little too young, and there might have been a reason for that.

One night, just months into this new monthly cycle, I confronted my mother about the travesty. The room was dark and she was alone; the TV glowed pale blue, holding her transfixed face in a gentle caress. I crawled into bed next to her, ready to interrogate her.

"How old were you when *you* got your first period?"

"Uhh, I think I was ten, like you."

I groaned. "So this is *your* fault. *You're* the reason I got mine early, too!"

She conceded that this might be true, and while I held tight to this absurd resentment for years, until my periods became more manageable as a teenager, it took far longer before I realized that I was a statistic, part of the increasing number of people who are starting their period at younger ages.

Several studies indicate that, across the board, people—particularly young girls—are starting puberty earlier. A *New York Times* article profiling precocious puberty noted that major pediatric institutions agree that girls' breasts are budding at younger ages; the most surprising finding was that by age seven, 23 percent of black girls have started developing breasts compared to just 10 percent of white girls, 15 percent of Latina girls, and 2 percent of Asian girls. The average age of starting menstruation declined dramatically in the twentieth century, probably because of better health and nutrition, but has mostly held steady at 12.5 years old in the United States for the last forty years. But it's worth noting that black American girls in particular tend to start their periods earlier than any other racial demographic. Theories abound as to why this is happening; some suggest childhood obesity can trigger puberty, while others suggest childhood stress, and both doctors and granola moms cite endocrine disruptors—chemical compounds that mimic estrogen, found in everything from pesticides to food—as potential culprits. Whatever the cause, puberty is becoming a reality for many of us once we're barely out of third or fourth grade. What does that mean for young black girls in America?

Short-term, starting puberty earlier can trigger hormonally charged mood swings and stress for young black girls who are ill equipped to handle PMS or the responsibility of menstruation. Couple that with the fact that black girls already face racist stigma regarding behavioral issues—young black girls are suspended and expelled from school at a higher rate than their peers—and you have a recipe for disaster: expectations of disruptive behavior based on racist stereotypes and actual inability to compartmentalize moody moments. One can be eleven years old with the body of a sixteen-year-old, but that doesn't mean they'll have a sixteen-year-old brain.

Another alarming factor of black girls developing early is the West's judgmental attitude toward them. According to a study conducted by the Georgetown Law's Center on Poverty and Inequality, adults view black girls as less innocent and requiring less nurturing and protection than white girls. Additionally, this study showed that adults view black girls' bodies as more grown and inherently sexual than white girls of the same age. Yes, there's a history of blatant desexualization as well, as seen in popular African American archetypes like the Mammy: kindly, unthreatening—and sex? Foreign concept. But I'm going to touch on the Jezebel archetype: promiscuous, deviant, fast, trouble. These are all descriptions that are far too often applied to young black girls. I mean, just a short perusal of social media exposes this; a group of black girls can't even post a video of themselves dancing without being called hoes and being subjected to respectability politics. Add a dash of early-onset puberty and, bam, even more sexual shame and perhaps even higher rates of sexual assault. Carolyn M. West touches on this in her essay "Mammy, Sapphire, and Jezebel: Historical Images of Black Women and Their Implications for Psychotherapy." She states that black women report a higher proportion of attempted sexual assault and that victim-blaming attitudes are often compounded for black women.

But wait, there's more: Starting your period at an early age can be a factor in health problems down the line. Research has shown that those who experience an early period are at a higher risk of developing breast cancer, diabetes, and heart disease; they also have a higher mortality rate if they develop ovarian cancer.

Great. It's not like being a black girl or woman in America isn't hard enough without worrying about sexual assault and cancer!

I'M STRUCK BY HOW I VIEWED MY EARLY PERIOD AS A TRUE CURSE, PASSED FROM MOTHER TO DAUGHTER. MORE SPECIFICALLY, *BLACK* MOTHER TO *BLACK* DAUGHTER, ALONG WITH THE OTHER SORDID REALITIES OF BLACK WOMANHOOD.

Don't get me wrong, I'm happy—*proud*—to be a black woman, and my days of resenting genetics for plaguing me with an early period and the calamity that came with it are long gone. I still think the girl in *Are You There God? It's Me, Margaret* was absolutely nuts for wanting her period so badly—can't relate, sis! I would have loved to start mine when I had a little more emotional maturity to deal with a tampon. But that beef with my mom's uterus is long gone. Still, I think back to that night as a child, in bed with my mom, the TV glow, my anguish, her helplessness . . . and I'm struck by how I viewed my early period as a true curse, passed from mother to daughter. More specifically, *black* mother to *black* daughter, along with the other sordid realities of black womanhood. I wonder if it's all some twisted rite of passage, passing the trauma torch with a dash of hormonal fuckery for added flavor. But maybe there's a way to make this less of a curse—less of a cataclysmic prelude to life as a black woman— and more of an opportunity to bring healthy awareness to the realities of what's to come. I don't have a blueprint on the least traumatic way to inform a young black girl about misogynistic anti-blackness or the discomfort of rocking a pad in elementary school. But if I have a daughter, I intend on finding a way to be transparent without being too horrifying. If she feels intimidated by the overwhelming menstrual maintenance, I'll assure her that it really does get better. If someone treats her body with disrespect, I'll assure her that her body isn't an object of shame. If she's unfairly deemed a troublemaker or a bad influence for merely speaking her mind or having the audacity to cop an attitude while she's PMSing, I'll assure her that she's not the monster this society thinks she is. It's not a cure-all—there isn't one—but all I can assure my daughter is support for her bloody, black, and hopefully bright future.

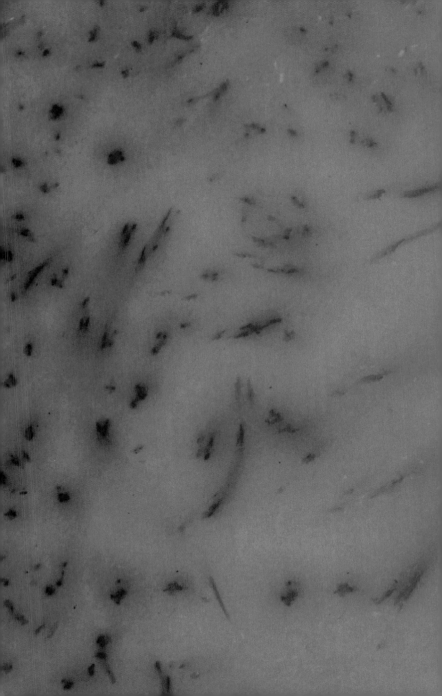

The Homeless Period:
It Doesn't Bear Thinking About and That's the Problem

KYLYSSA SHAY

There are a lot of things I'd rather forget about from my time spent being homeless; my menstrual periods are certainly one of them. Periods aren't particularly pleasant to put up with anyway, but adding the complication of homelessness brings inconvenience to the level of misery.

Human beings prefer to be clean. It affects how they feel, physically and emotionally, and how people treat them. Having a period while homeless is more disturbing, upsetting, and crude than having a period while homed and possessed of all the gleaming white cotton and superabsorbent miracles modern society has to offer.

On the street, it's also an unpleasant reminder of vulnerability. Nothing else so absolutely ordinary reminds you that you have a vagina—something other people are quite willing to viciously harm you for—quite like having a period while homeless. When you've suffered indignity heaped upon indignity compounded by lack of sleep and the apparent absence of all human love from your world, the only thing you can realistically hope to hang on to is a desire to handle what you can't avoid with grace.

TOILET PAPER DOESN'T
CUT IT, FOLKS

People with uteruses have been dealing with blood, fluids, and tissue coming from between their legs since before *Homo sapiens* were even a thing. They have used moss, feathers, leaves, wool, natural fibers, old cloth, milkweed fluff, and probably dozens of other things to soak up their monthly spills of uterine lining. So you'd think toilet paper would be the Holy Grail compared to an old handkerchief or a wad of reindeer moss. It is and it isn't.

The toilet paper you have in your home has been gently handled since you've gotten it, hasn't it? It hasn't gotten wet and it certainly hasn't gotten dirty. That stuff wouldn't be too bad for swabbing below the decks and plugging any leaks. It's still a pain in the arse to keep in place when used as a sanitary napkin and not easy to remove when used as a tampon.

But the toilet paper homeless women have access to isn't nice toilet paper; it isn't your toilet paper. It's often stored open in dirty back rooms or alleys. It's been lugged around and set down anywhere before the maintenance person gets it to the restroom.

HAVING A PERIOD WHILE HOMELESS IS MORE DISTURBING, UPSETTING, AND CRUDE THAN HAVING A PERIOD WHILE HOMED AND POSSESSED OF ALL THE GLEAMING WHITE COTTON AND SUPERABSORBENT MIRACLES MODERN SOCIETY HAS TO OFFER.

After it's been installed, it's been touched by strangers who've gotten feces, urine, or menstrual blood on their hands. It also receives a filthy baptism of vaporized dirty toilet water on it every time someone flushes.

You don't even want to wipe with public bathroom toilet roll anymore now, do you? Imagine that definitely nonsanitary stuff making rude contact with the lady parts of someone you love. The vagina is like the perfect warm, moist petri dish for growing all the bacteria that public restroom toilet paper brings to the panty party.

IRREGULAR ACCESS TO BATHROOMS

So public bathrooms aren't perfect, but they do tend to have running water and a small amount of privacy. Unfortunately, most homeless people lack safe, reliable access to bathrooms for many reasons. Businesses close, government buildings close, public toilets close, and homeless shelter bathrooms have lines and other restrictions, assuming one can get into a shelter in the first place and chooses to do so. Showers are even harder to get access to than toilets. When they are available, they're often as unsanitary as the average gas station bathroom in a bad neighborhood, and may cost money to use. If you can't get a shower but once a week, you may start to develop a less-than-fresh feeling in your nether regions when the red tide comes in.

PADS AND TAMPONS COST MONEY . . . AND SO DOES FOOD

We all have to make choices, but some of them are just too hard to properly prioritize when one is sleep-deprived, hungry, dirty, and blorping out bodily fluids that need hygienic disposal. Menstruating homeless people find themselves with a nasty joke of a math story problem, and it has no correct answer, only slightly less wrong ones, often when they're in no state of mind to make good choices even if there were any. I'll admit, I considered shoplifting tampons when I was homeless. With less than a dollar in my pocket, there was no way I could buy them. But I could also imagine all too well how upsetting it would be to be arrested for stealing tampons.

HOMELESS PEOPLE HAVE LIMITED WARDROBES

If you get a bit of red on your designated period panties, you can change into another pair and spray the dirty ones with stain remover or even toss them in the sink for a wash. But a homeless woman will quickly run out of changes of whatever item of clothing gets stained if she has to carry all her possessions around with her. Those little period accidents are also a lot less frequent when you have access to enough pads or tampons to change them as often as needed.

LACK OF SLEEP AND ROUGH SLEEPING INCREASES CRAMPING, PAIN, FATIGUE, AND HEADACHES

A homed woman can go to bed at night with a heating pad or hot-water bottle and an overnight pad with wings stuck in her most comfy granny panties. She can take a Midol, maybe have a cup of hot tea and a nibble of dark chocolate, and go off to sleep in comfort in her favorite jammies.

A homeless woman may not be able to sleep at night at all because she's on constant alert for predators. She may already be sore from sleeping on the ground, and she has no hot-water bottle and no cupboard with a bottle of Midol and a selection of teas in it. Homelessness almost guarantees sleep deprivation, which is proven to harm pain processing.

HOW ABOUT HELPING OUT?

It would have been a kind thing if anyone had helped me out with period products when I was homeless. No one did, but you can do it for someone else.

You can help the homeless people in your area deal with periods by donating pads, tampons, hand sanitizer, and cleansing wipes to your local homeless charities and food banks. You can also make and distribute hygiene kits yourself.

WHAT TO PUT IN A PERIOD KIT

There are a number of options when it comes to making period care kits for people with insufficient access to running water. All kits should contain hand sanitizer and cleansing wipes. There are a few choices to make after that.

I've given examples of a few different kinds of kits to give you some ideas of how to make up a few yourself, if you so choose. Please keep in mind that these are just ideas and however you use them is good.

These kits can be assembled in quart- or gallon-sized Ziploc bags to keep their contents safe and dry.

#1 Super Basic Street Period Kit

hand sanitizer

cleansing wipes

a package of pads or a package of tampons

#2 Kit Idea

hand sanitizer

cleansing wipes

a package of pads

a package of tampons

#3 Kit Idea

hand sanitizer

cleansing wipes

a package of pads

a package of tampons

a pack of panty liners

a bottle of pain reliever

#4 More Eco-Conscious Kit Idea

hand sanitizer

cleansing wipes

a menstrual cup

printed instructions for use

THE TYPES OF PADS, TAMPONS, AND OTHER HEALTH AND HYGIENE ITEMS I THINK ARE BEST FOR THESE KITS AND WHY

PADS:

The thin, individually wrapped pads with wings are the best all-around choice for pads to include in a care package for homeless people. They are less likely to chafe when a person is doing a lot of walking, and the wings help them stay stuck to panties through a lot of moving about. They also work for light or heavy days, and the individual wrappers help protect the pads and keep them clean until they're ready to be used. Overnight pads that are longer may also be advantageous because they provide more coverage, reducing the possibility of leaks.

TAMPONS:

While tampons without applicators may be

better for the environment, they are a bit dicey to insert with fingers that may not be sparkling clean and minty fresh. So I'd highly recommend tampons with applicators that are individually wrapped in plastic to keep them clean and pristine as new-fallen snow until needed.

PANTY LINERS:

Any individually wrapped, unscented panty liner with decent adhesive that covers most of the bottom of the liner is a good thing. Liners with very little adhesive coverage have a tendency to come loose, so they should be avoided. Scented liners can irritate and may not smell good to the person who gets them. Scented liners also may serve as a reminder that another choice has been made for you in an already out-of-control world.

MENSTRUAL CUPS:

Any menstrual cup that's made of silicone and has an easy-to-grip removal stem would be a good choice. Silicone is good because the cup can be heat-sterilized if necessary; it's pliable and long-lasting, too. Cups that come with sturdy storage containers are always a plus.

HAND SANITIZER:

I recommend getting the clear, unscented hand sanitizer that comes in pocket-sized bottles without any colored plastic beads in it. Those plastic beads aren't doing the environment any favors and nobody wants to find little sparkly bits on their sanitary napkin.

WIPES:

Forget the branded feminine wipes; get flushable wet toilet wipes instead. Those little feminine wipe packets seldom have enough cleansing liquid in them, and the wipes inside are often tiny, folded things textured like hand wipes. The wipes intended to help people wipe their bottoms cleaner in the bathroom are bigger and softer and much better at cleaning things up. The unscented kind of whatever wipe you get is best, as some people are sensitive or even allergic to scents, especially when used near delicate skin areas.

PERIOD PAIN RELIEVER:

Pamprin, Midol, Tylenol, Advil, and their generics are all pretty good for relieving menstrual pain. While one of the formulas intended for menstrual pain relief, like Midol or Pamprin, would probably be the most welcome, any pain reliever would be a blessing.

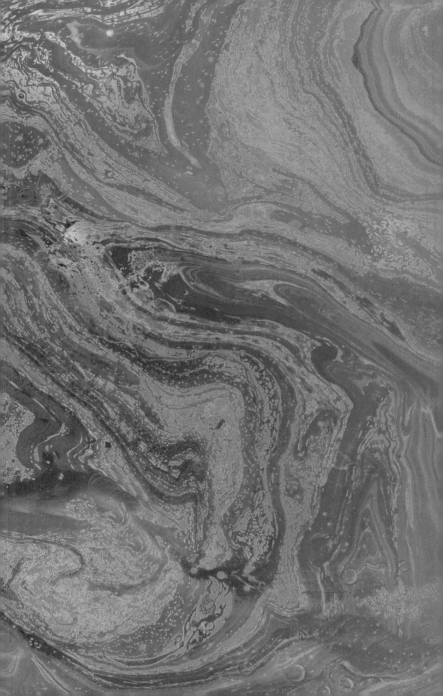

Bad Blood

EMMA STRAUB

I got my first period the day before my eleventh birthday. I'd been lying about it for months, saying that it had already come, because one of the other girls in my very small middle-school class got her period before I did, and I was jealous. Menstruating seemed so adult, so womanly, that it was downright sexy. But there it was, finally! My mother had an elegant friend who had taken her daughter for tea at the Plaza to celebrate her first period, and so we did that, too. Instead of feeling like Eloise—who was, after all, a child—I felt like a movie star.

In high school, when other girls began to bleed unexpectedly, they always came to me, knowing that I had a stash of tampons on my person that would last most women several months. Super-plus tampons, super tampons, regular tampons, bulky pads, panty liners, Advil—I had it all. The period I had so desperately wanted had not only arrived, it had arrived with force. The folded-paper instruction manual that came with each enormous box of tampons claimed that a normal menstrual flow was about two ounces of blood per month. I felt like I lost that much in an hour. Every trip to the doctor ended with her telling me that I was terribly anemic, which I knew. How could I not be? The blood was leaving my body at such a high rate that I was surprised there was any left for her to take.

Once, one of my male friends' younger sisters came up to me in the lobby of our school. She was a freshman, and I was a senior. "I've had a tampon in for two days," she said. "I forgot about it." She looked at me for advice, perhaps because I was older and wiser, but also, I presume, because she knew I was some kind of menstrual oracle. I couldn't imagine leaving a tampon in for more than two hours, let alone two days. My own period was already so bad—the cramps, the bleeding—that I'd gone on the birth control pill to try to beat it into submission.

It was the end of high school by the time I realized that bleeding every month sucked, and it quickly went from "sucked" to "actually ruining my life." The birth control pills worked for a while—my cramps improved, but the bleeding was still heavy. Every few months, my college roommate came home with a new box of Tampax slenders, tampons that I could make expand just by looking at them. Meanwhile, I doubled up on pads and supers, and bled through onto my sheets anyway, easily going through one large box of supplies during every period, if not more. I'd had some sporty-ish friends, the kind of people who wanted to play intramural softball or pick-up basketball, or go camping, during that time of the month, and my first thought was always: "How can you do anything that is so far away from a bathroom? How can you be so cavalier?" My period lasted a solid week, if not more, heavy for the first few days, and heavier than most people's normal periods even on my lightest days. I knew every single bathroom on my college campus intimately.

As I got older, I'd look at my schedule and cringe when I saw that I was due for my period, knowing how much harder it would make everything I'm supposed to do. (Taking the subway to work for forty minutes? Impossible. I can't be away from a bathroom for that long.) I'd fill my purse with pills and supplies, wear my oldest, darkest underwear, and hope for the best. The feeling is like boarding an airplane when you know there's going to be extreme turbulence. The ride is going to be bumpy, but you have no choice but to get on board.

A couple of years ago, I went off the pill for the first time in over a decade. Though intellectually I understood that the hormones in the pills had been controlling my period, it was nonetheless a shock to see the change. My period went from heavy-but-not-completely-insane to the hallway scene in *The Shining*. And because I realized how much garbage I was producing every month—all those applicators, all those cardboard boxes, all those little plastic sleeves—I'd switched to a hippie option, the DivaCup, which my friends swore by. One friend told me it was so great, she'd empty it once or twice a day, and that was it! She practically had stars in her eyes. I was sold.

You know the phrase "my cup runneth over"? Not to be disgusting, but my cup ranneth over every half hour. I was traveling a lot at the time, with the band I work for and doing research for my novel, and sometimes I would be in transit all day long, timing my bathroom-stop requests as far apart as I could, waiting until the last second to board airplanes, running through gas stations because I didn't want to ruin one of only a few dresses in my suitcase. I sprinted into filthy bathrooms, into Porta-Potties, into places I would usually avoid like the plague. Waiting for a clean spot (ideally, my own bathroom) just wasn't an option.

The blood was everywhere. It was on my clothes, on my skin, on the toilet bowl, on the bathroom floor. I couldn't control it, not with Advil or with expensive pills from my gynecologist that were supposed to stanch my flow. Or rather, the pills worked—they cut the bleeding by a third on the heaviest days—but a third of a monsoon is still a monsoon. I went for dinner at a friend's house and sat on her beautiful vintage chaise lounge, because she asked me to, because she knew I'd love it, and then did nothing but think about the possibility of ruining it all night long. I left work early,

I left parties early, and I canceled plans left and right. On my heaviest days, I had half an hour between visits to the bathroom, if I was lucky. I got no sleep, even with an old towel tucked underneath my body, just in case. Each period lasted more than a week, sometimes two, and left me feeling like I'd been through a war. Even though most people with functional ovaries between the ages of approximately twelve and fifty-one menstruate, most of them don't have to worry about the shame of having an accident, the weird looks from friends and coworkers when you excuse yourself every thirty minutes, and all that blood.

People loved to give advice. One friend recommended I try acupuncture, which I'd done before and had helped with other physical ailments. I took herbal remedies, and of course iron, so much iron. The acupuncture was fine, until I bled through my clothes on the table, leaving a small round stain behind, and then drove myself home crying, knowing I wouldn't make it home fast enough to avoid another accident.

After a year of this, I finally went to a new doctor. What took me so long, I have no idea. I think I always assumed that this was just my cross to bear, that nothing could be done, that it wasn't that bad. Never mind that I had never—never—met anyone with periods like mine. Because I'd always been healthy, it truly never occurred to me that there could be any actual problem. It took visits to several specialists, but finally, after months (which, of course, meant more periods) my new doctor (also known as my queen, my goddess, my deliverer from evil) discovered the gigantic colony of fibroids that had been wreaking havoc on my uterus. My doctor explained them to me like this: A normal uterus squeezes itself every month, contracting to rid itself of its lining. She squeezed her fist together, the way you'd squeeze a lemon. When you have a fibroid, a non-cancerous cyst, it can interfere with normal uterine contractions, and so the bleeding can't regulate itself—the uterus wants to keep squeezing and squeezing, shedding more and more blood. This summer, I had two surgeries to remove them—one giant monster fibroid and then several little baby-monster fibroids, too many to count, like Gremlins.

I THINK IT'S A GOOD LESSON ABOUT KNOWING YOUR OWN BODY—IF SOMETHING SEEMS LIKE IT'S FUCKED UP, IT PROBABLY IS.

The surgeries weren't bad—I got to go home afterward—and I was pretty much back to normal within a week. I was lucky in this regard—some people have far more invasive surgeries, depending on the position of the fibroid. Friends sent me boxes of snacks and comic books and flowers, and my husband took excellent care of me, sweetly hopeful that the worst was behind us. My only regret is that I waited so long to figure out what was wrong. I think it's a good lesson about knowing your own body—if something seems like it's fucked up, it probably is. I don't think I'll ever be reluctant to call a doctor again.

There are, of course, reasons why having your period is a good thing. I would never have gone on those pills that reduce your period to four times a year, because that just seems weird to me. The clockwork regularity of my period is comforting to me—it's satisfying to know that my body's doing its thing just fine. Having your period is also a great way to know that you're not pregnant, which can be very reassuring. For obvious reasons, I'm way, way past the point of seeing any charm whatsoever in my monthly visitor, but I know that it's a minor inconvenience for most people. I wish that I still felt as excited about that particular part of becoming an adult as I did when I was in junior high school.

Though it's still early to tell for sure, my life seems to have improved. I've had one fairly normal period. I still know all the best public bathrooms in the city (if you're in downtown Manhattan, forget the Apple Store, and go to Room & Board—trust me). I still carry enough feminine products to act as a dam in a pinch, though with the DivaCup now able to handle my flow, I need them more just for my own peace of mind. The fibroids will almost certainly grow back, so my reprieve might be short-lived, but I'm happy to take what I can get. It was so bad for so long, I don't quite believe that the blood is gone forever. Every month, I'll cross my fingers and hope for the best, and if it gets really debilitating again, I won't wait another month before going back to the doctor. I'm not going to join any swim teams in the meantime, or hike up Mount Kilimanjaro, but who knows—I might have a whole three weeks of freedom. It's a start.

The Politics of Periods

JENNIFER WEISS-WOLF

Menstruation is having a moment—surfing the crimson wave of fame, so to speak. Quite a stark contrast to my own teenage years in the 1980s, when periods were mentioned in whispers (the word wasn't actually spoken on TV until 1985!), tampons kept under wraps, and cramps quietly endured. Going public with the discussion has been downright liberating—a welcome and long-overdue advance.

NOW THE TIME IS RIPE TO HARNESS ALL THAT MOMENTUM AND GO FULL-BLOWN POLITICAL: PERIODS AS A PUBLIC POLICY AGENDA.

And just look how far we've come. After an explosion of rebellious activism and innovation in 2015, NPR designated it "the Year of the Period." *Cosmopolitan* magazine declared we've entered the era of "Period Power." An oversized torpedo-like tampon was featured on the April 29, 2016, cover of *Newsweek* with the headline "There Will Be

Blood. (Get Over It.) Period Stigma Is Hurting the Economy, Schools and the Environment. But the Crimson Tide Is Turning." And actress Ashley Judd even gave a worldwide shout-out to period activism at the Women's March in January 2017 by performing the poem "Nasty Woman" by Nina Donovan.

Given that this particular bodily function has been an essential slice of the human condition forever—and stigmatized, sidelined, or, at best, ignored for just about as long—it is no small thrill that menstruation has become a modern cause célèbre.

Now the time is ripe to harness all that momentum and go full-blown political: periods as a public policy agenda. It is what I call the fight for menstrual equity. What does that mean? In order to have a fully participatory society, we must have laws and policies that ensure menstrual products are safe and affordable for everyone who needs them. The ability to access these items affects a person's freedom to work, study, stay healthy, and engage in the world with basic dignity. And if anyone's access is compromised, whether by poverty or stigma or lack of education and resources, it is in *all* of our interests to ensure those needs are met.

As hard as it may be to believe, for millions in America today—those living paycheck to paycheck, or without a paycheck at all, or on the streets, or in government custody—tampons and pads can be an impossible luxury. A year's supply costs in the range of $70 to $120. This can be an out-of-reach expense for many—possibly even the difference between making rent and putting food on the table. Other reusable alternatives like menstrual cups, cloth pads, and period underwear can be cost-effective over time (more environmentally friendly, too) but require a steep upfront investment.

WELCOME TO THE FIGHT FOR MENSTRUAL EQUITY.

There's some painful bias to these statistics as well, making periods doubly burdensome for those who are poorest. While middle-class families can take advantage of options like bulk discounts or shopping at wholesale retailers to buy a supply of tampons, those who live in poverty end up paying considerably more for the exact same items, whether it is because they're subject to inflated prices at convenience stores or are only able to expend precious dollars one necessity at a time. For those who are homeless or incarcerated, monthly bleeding is especially brutal. The most commonly reported substitutes when maxi pads aren't in the budget? Newspaper, brown paper bags, old rags, and socks.

Access to affordable menstrual products is a necessity for half the population. Yet this reality is given practically *zero* consideration in the laws by which we live. Think about this: Tampons and pads are ineligible for purchases made with public benefits like food stamps; they're not made routinely available in shelters or crisis centers, nor are they provided in any uniform way in jails and prisons. In the vast majority of states, menstrual products are not even exempt from sales tax, forcing the customer to pay added cents on the dollar. And while the government regulates the provision of toilet paper and hand soap—requiring these in public restrooms, including in schools and workplaces—we're on our own when it comes to managing our periods.

Outraged yet? I hope so! Welcome to the fight for menstrual equity. The good news is that in every single one of these instances, thoughtful policy change *can* make a difference. Here are some of the new laws that are being advanced across the country.

THE TAMPON TAX

The fight to eliminate sales tax on menstrual products—better known as the tampon tax— has caught on around the world. The core argument for scrapping the tax: The products we use to manage our periods qualify as a "necessity of life" and therefore are worthy of a sales tax exemption. Here in the United States, among the items that most states already include in this category are food and medicine—which means that even things like

Fruit Roll-Ups, Pop-Tarts, and ChapStick get a tax break.

If you think it sounds crazy that we even have to make the case that tampons be classified as a necessity or deemed as indispensable as a bag of chips, you're not alone. Prior to 2015, forty of the fifty states collected taxes on menstrual products; of those other ten states, only five were ahead of the curve and had already begun exempting menstrual products (Maryland, Massachusetts, Minnesota, New Jersey, and Pennsylvania); the other five (Alaska, Delaware, Montana, New Hampshire, and Oregon) collect no sales tax at all.

Since then, thanks to a nationwide petition and campaign, a whopping twenty-four states have introduced legislation to scrap the tampon tax. Even more heartening, lawmakers from both sides of the aisle are getting behind the cause, Democrats and Republicans alike, making menstruation one of the rare, truly bipartisan matters in American politics.

So far, three states—Florida, Illinois, and New York—have succeeded in passing and implementing new laws to make menstrual products entirely tax-free. The city of Chicago and District of Columbia passed ordinances to the same effect. And Connecticut removed sales tax revenue from menstrual products from its 2018 statewide budget, effectively eliminating the tax.

TAMPONS FOR ALL

Beyond the sales tax, there is an increasingly widespread belief that menstrual products should even be free—or at least made more affordable and accessible—for those who are most in need. In terms of practical relief for families that are struggling and truly unable to meet the monthly expense of these items, a tax savings isn't going to make enough of a dent. There is more we can do.

New York City has proudly led the way. In 2016, it unanimously passed three ground-breaking laws that mandate the provision of free tampons and pads for all the city's public schools, shelters, and jails—the most comprehensive legislation of its kind in the world. Los Angeles followed the Big Apple's lead in 2017 and passed an ordinance requiring free access to tampons in all county juvenile detention centers; Colorado did so for all of its state prisons. Similar laws are being introduced in many states across the country, from California to Connecticut.

Capitol Hill is also making waves. Debating periods in the hallowed halls of Congress? That's a first—and a very big deal! But it is happening. US Sentators Cory Booker and Elizabeth Warren demanded free menstrual products for federal prisoners with the introduction of the Dignity for Incarcerated Women Act. And US Representative Grace Meng introduced the Menstrual Equity for All Act of 2017, the first-ever federal menstrual access bill. Among its provisions, the bill would:

1. Allow individuals to buy menstrual products with money they contribute to pre-tax flexible spending accounts;

2. Provide a refundable tax credit to low-income individuals for the purchase of menstrual products;

3. Enable federal grant funds to be used by homeless assistance providers

to make available menstrual products, along with other allowable essentials like soap and toothpaste;

4. Require that menstrual products be freely available to incarcerated inmates and detainees; and

5. Mandate that large employers provide menstrual products to employees in workplace restrooms.

Meanwhile, dozens of college campuses across the country—from NYU to UCLA and the University of Nebraska to the University of Arizona—have taken up the cause as well. Students have lobbied administrations or leveraged funds to ensure access for all. At Grinnell College, in Iowa, one intrepid student initiated a campus-wide caper that launched a powerful protest. She used bobby pins to break open campus dispensers, freeing all the tampons and pads for others to use. "I freed your tampons kept behind lock, key, and quarter," she wrote in a public letter to the college. "Bleeding bodies deserve to think about Foucault and micro-organisms and the history of the bleeding bodies that came before them. When we menstruate, however unexpectedly, we should not feel fear in the pits of our stomachs because of your lack of foresight. We are a part of this college. Provide free menstrual products to students who need them so I can stop picking the locks on your bogus machines." The president of Grinnell, a former deputy director of the National Institutes of Health, agreed. "It's not unreasonable to provide free menstrual products everywhere, including on campuses," he announced. "We have free toilet paper, so wanting the same for menstrual products is not extreme. This is a normal human function." Indeed.

THE FUTURE OF MENSTRUAL EQUITY

Even with this progress, many other critical fights for women's health and rights continue to be waged at all levels of government—from statehouses to Congress, and all the way up to the US Supreme Court.

Which is *exactly* why I believe menstruation belongs smack in the middle of policy-making. Our periods, quite amazingly, are a potent rallying force. We are half the population and must leverage our collective voice and power. It is up to us to make menstruation a mainstream matter: It is not a secret; we deserve to have our basic needs met, and we should not be made to feel ashamed.

How can we be political about periods? It's actually remarkably simple. Talk about it. Tweet about it. Write about it. Whether you prefer to craft poetry or prose, publish a letter to the editor, or petition your school principal—or even the president of the United States—it all makes a difference.

Let's push our leaders to make menstrual equity a priority. At a minimum, that includes championing policies that prioritize the immediate needs of those who menstruate: access, affordability, safety. In so doing, we can recognize and elevate the power, pride—and absolute normalcy—of periods. It is a fight that stands to improve all our lives.

Periods, According to Pop Culture

ELIZABETH YUKO

Every family is different, and talking about periods is no exception. Some people discuss menstruation with a family member or friend before puberty even starts. Others will learn about how the female reproductive system works in school or from looking information up on their own. But before most people get The Talk or do their first Google search, they're given clues about how menstruation works from popular culture.

ASK **ANY WOMAN** WHO CAME OF AGE BETWEEN THE 1970S AND 1990S TO NAME THEIR **FIRST MEMORY** OF PERIODS IN POP CULTURE AND, CHANCES ARE, A LOT OF THEM WILL MENTION **JUDY BLUME**'S 1970 NOVEL *ARE YOU THERE GOD? IT'S ME, MARGARET.*

Our first exposure is typically advertisements on TV, where we're offered small, inaccurate clues about what periods are like. If we believed what we saw on commercials, we'd think period blood is blue and wearing tampons magically gives you the ability to ride a horse or scale a mountain on a bike (as much as I'd love to take credit for this observation, it's been around for quite a while, notably appearing in *Pulling Our Own Strings* (1980), an anthology of feminist humor and satire). In reality, it's bright red, much thicker than water, can include dark-colored blood clots, and doesn't make you any more skilled in outdoor activities. If this isn't something you're prepared for, it can be unsettling and scary. After being taught all our lives that blood is the sign that something's wrong, all of a sudden we're expected to be perfectly fine with bleeding involuntarily in our underwear a few days a month. It goes against everything we know, and it's completely normal for it to take a while to get used to this.

THANKS, MARGARET (AND JUDY!)

Ask any woman who came of age between the 1970s and 1990s to name their first memory of periods in pop culture and, chances are, a lot of them will mention Judy Blume's 1970 novel *Are You There God? It's Me, Margaret.* In the book, Margaret and her friends anxiously anticipate their first periods, ultimately walking the reader through the ups and downs of Margaret's experience. For a lot of us, this was our introduction to periods. Sure, by the time I read it in the early 1990s, there were mentions of periods on TV and in the movies, but there was something extra private and secure about being able to read it in a book, at your own time and pace—rereading the same dog-eared pages to make sure you absorb it all before having to return the book to the library.

Another notable menstruation mention actually came five years earlier in *The Long Secret* (the 1965 sort-of sequel to *Harriet* the Spy, by Louise Fitzhugh). Although the book isn't as inextricably linked to periods as Margaret, they are an important topic of conversation between Harriet and her friends Beth Ellen and Janie. Thanks to learning about periods from her Victorian grandmother, Beth Ann was under the impression that the bleeding was caused by rocks passing through her reproductive system. Janie puts an end to that rumor, reassuring Beth Ann and Harriet that that's not what happens, and goes on to explain, in scientific detail, what actually happens during menstruation—disposal of the unused uterine lining and all. She also tells the girls that she's working on developing a "cure" for periods (specifically for women who don't want to have children), and that there is a (minor) upside to the monthly inconvenience: getting out of gym class.

FIRST PERIODS: LIKE IT OR NOT, YOU'RE A WOMAN NOW

First periods are usually shown as momentous occasions—a transition into "womanhood" (whatever that means). For some people it is. For others, it's not. If you get your period and you feel completely different, more power to you. If you get your period and feel exactly the same, only now bleed once a month, that's fine, too. If you get your period but don't identify as a woman, that's also a thing.

As Lauren Rosewarne discusses in her excellent 2012 book *Periods in Pop Culture*, the only place people are ever really comfortable with periods—and even here, "comfortable" is a stretch—is in a bathroom. This provides both privacy for the menstruating person as well as physical separation from men. It also suggests that periods are in the same category as other bathroom functions, like urinating or pooping: something gross that you can control. This comes up in the 2007 movie *Superbad* when Jonah Hill's character gets upset when "someone period-ed" on his leg—as if it was something intentional and controllable.

IF YOU GET YOUR PERIOD AND YOU FEEL **COMPLETELY DIFFERENT**, MORE POWER TO YOU. IF YOU GET YOUR PERIOD AND FEEL EXACTLY THE SAME, ONLY NOW BLEED ONCE A MONTH, THAT'S FINE, TOO.

Not everyone has had the benefit of TV and films for learning about periods. In three "period period pieces"—representations of menstruation on-screen taking place in the past—characters each think they're dying when they get their first period. In *My Girl* (which came out in 1991 but took place in 1972), Vada (Anna Chlumsky) screams and tells her father's girlfriend that she's "hemorrhaging" when she first spots period blood. In *Dr. Quinn, Medicine Woman* (which aired from 1993–1998 and was set in the 1860s) and *Anne with an E* (based on L. M. Montgomery's beloved Anne of Green Gables books, aired in 2017 and set in the 1890s), the characters of Colleen (Jessica Bowman) and Anne (Amybeth McNulty), respectively, think they're dying when they first notice their periods. In all three situations, each of the characters' mothers are dead and were not able to fill their daughters in on the ins and outs of menstruation, resulting in them believing they were dying.

In each of those shows, the characters eventually learn that menstruating is completely normal. That also happens in another period period piece—*Mad Men* (2007–2015)—Sally Draper (Kiernan Skipka), who is not particularly close with her mother, runs home to see her after getting her first period in the natural history museum. Her mother tells her that this is normal and means that "everything is working." Similarly, in *Roseanne* (1988–1997; 2018), Darlene Conner (Sara Gilbert) gets her first period at the age of eleven and worries that it means that she'll no longer be able to play baseball and instead will have to do things like wear panty hose. Her mother assures her that it doesn't, telling her that "it's almost magical" and that she "should be really proud today 'cause this is the beginning of a lot of really wonderful things in your life." And just to keep it real, she acknowledges that cramps are also part of the deal.

Pop culture also tells us that there is no equivalent of getting a first period for boys. In *My Girl*, Vada says, "It's not fair. Nothing happens to boys." Along the same lines, in *Anne with an E*, Anne asks her classmates, "Do boys have to contend with anything like this?" Both characters feel unprepared and almost betrayed that their entry into adulthood is marked by blood and pain. Boys, on the other hand, are typically shown during puberty with voices dropping, masturbation, and wet dreams—none of which involve an element of pain and, if anything, are pleasurable or positive experiences.

A CURSE TO BE FEARED

Even though certain books, TV shows, and movies talk about periods, it doesn't always involve characters assuring others that menstruating is normal and not something to be feared. For instance, variations of the man-to-man advice "never trust anything that can bleed for X days and not die" can be found throughout pop culture, including in *South Park: Bigger, Longer & Uncut* (1999). This idea positions menstruating women as creatures to be afraid of—dishonest and full of mysterious powers, likely used to the detriment of men—maybe even something inhuman. As Rosewarne points out, in 1976's *Carrie*, the titular character obtains her telekinetic abilities during her first period; two years prior, Regan, Linda Blair's character in *The Exorcist*, gets her powers—and possessed by the devil—as her period approaches. In some cases, fathers see it as their duty to educate their sons on the horrors of menstruation. In an episode of *Roseanne*, Dan Conner (John Goodman) finds his son, D.J. (Michael Fishman), running upstairs screaming. When

Dan asks D.J. what's wrong, D.J. tells him that his mother (Roseanne) was telling him about her period, to which Dan responds: "As you were"—implying that menstruation is so terrifying and horrific that it warrants running away and panicked shrieking. And it's not just men who are taught to fear periods, as Blanche Devereaux (Rue McClanahan) demonstrated in an episode of *The Golden Girls* (1985–1992). She explains that she was terrified of The Curse, and only learned what it was two years *after* getting her period.

OUT, DAMNED SPOT

If periods are something men should fear because of the supposed supernatural powers that come along with them, women learn early on that we should be terrified of any visible stains during our period—a very public dead giveaway of this otherwise private bodily function. In *Anne with an E*, one of Anne Shirley's classmates tells her that she stays home from school when she has her period out of fear of having an accident like someone else in their school did, instilling the fear of visible leakage in Anne, who places her hands behind her back the next time she stands up to answer a question in class.

A rare exception to this is in an episode of *Broad City* (2014–) when Ilana Wexler (Ilana Glazer) wears jeans with a very obvious period bloodstain while traveling in order to get through airport security without any TSA agents conducting a thorough-enough search to locate the marijuana she is bringing on the trip. In this case, Ilana turns this common plot point on its head, triumphantly using her period-stained pants—and the fact that most people find them disgusting—to her advantage. Another advance in talking about this aspect of periods, although the scene doesn't actually show period stains, is found in an episode of *Girls* (2012–2017). Hannah Horvath (Lena Dunham) tells her friend that she never knows when she's going to get her period, so it's always a surprise and is why her underwear are "covered in weird stains." Even though as an audience we don't *see* blood, the fact that Hannah is openly discussing these stains with her friend—as just another part of being in her twenties—destigmatizes the supposed horror we're supposed to feel around having an "accident." This also shows that even if you've been getting your period for several years, it doesn't mean you won't find yourself in a situation where you end up with unwanted underwear stains; this is just another normal thing that happens to a lot of people.

READ (OR WATCH) INSTRUCTIONS CAREFULLY

Despite the fact that Blume's classic *Are You There God? It's Me, Margaret* was published in 1970, it has served as "Periods 101" for generations of women—myself included. What was infinitely easier than asking someone else about periods? Reading about them myself. This was one of the most checked-out and visibly-worn books in my Catholic elementary school library in rural Ohio. Reading it was a rite of passage, but it wasn't only about Margaret's fictional experience with her first period: For a lot of us, it was also an instruction manual, albeit in some cases, a very outdated one. In the first edition of the book, Blume describes the equipment Margaret used to handle her period, which involved a complicated system of pads, pins, belts, and hooks that frankly sounded like a medieval torture device when I was reading the book in the early 1990s (despite its being a popular book, our school library still had the original version). Turns out, Blume wrote in a 2011 post on her blog, pads became the norm a few months after *Margaret* was published, making the book immediately outdated. Although—at the suggestion of her editor—Blume had Margaret using modern pads in subsequent editions, the wildly popular first edition was already out there, along with the pins and belts. I imagine I wasn't the only girl who was terribly confused—and also relieved—upon receiving a self-adhesive pad from my mother when I first got my period.

Even when periods are mentioned in other forms of pop culture, it's rare that instructions and specifics, like the ones found in *Margaret*, are included. There are at least two notable exceptions to this, though—one of which is in a highly unlikely show for which the target audience is not prepubescent girls. It came in an episode of *Curb Your Enthusiasm* (2000–) when a Girl Scout comes to Larry David's (Larry David) door selling cookies, at which time she gets her first period. In the show, Larry David plays a somewhat fictionalized version of himself—an awkward man in his sixties whose everyday life provides an opportunity to comment on various aspects of society (typically, the ones he finds most annoying). In other words, he's not the most obvious character on television to be dealing with menstruation, let alone a girl's first period. In this episode, David assures the Scout that she had her first period "in the right place" and runs upstairs to retrieve a tampon box his ex-wife left behind after she moved out. He gives her a tampon, but she doesn't know how to use it, so he stands outside the (closed) door and reads out the instructions that came with the box, step-by-step, walking her through the process until she gets it in. In this case, you have a character (David) literally telling another character—and in turn, the viewers—how to insert a tampon.

Another example came in an episode of *Anne with an E*, when the titular character gets her first period. Book purists—or those faithful to the beloved 1985 CBC film adaptation—will be quick to point out that this was never described or shown in previous versions, but given the fact that the story centers around a girl's adolescence and coming of age, it makes sense. Just after the opening credits, Anne is shown waking up in the middle of the night, startled, and running downstairs to heat water and wash her bedlinens. The camera pans to the washbasin, where a large bloodstain on white sheets clarifies that she's gotten her first period. Marilla Cuthbert (Geraldine James)—Anne's mother figure—finds Anne and tells her not to panic because this is a normal part of becoming a woman. She goes on to give Anne instructions on what to do: pin cotton cloths to her undergarments and wash them—first in cold water, then in hot water. Like in *Margaret*, this scene describes an outdated menstrual product, but the same method for washing period-bloodstained fabric that my mother taught me. Watching this in 2017, most of the audience will likely know that we've moved past pinning cloths to underwear, but at the same time, could benefit from the useful stain-removing tip.

TIMING IS EVERYTHING, APPARENTLY

Another aspect of menstruation that makes regularly scheduled appearances on television is the notion of periods being well, regularly scheduled. This can take the form of the myth of period synching—that a group of women who spend a lot of time together could end up on the same cycles—as well as the idea that these cycles can be used to keep track of time, or more frequently, the time of the month when male characters should be wary of ones who menstruate.

Let's start with some facts: This whole concept of period synching first came about from a 1971 study (www.nature.com/nature /journal/v229/n5282/abs/229244a0.html) that tracked the cycles of just 135 women living in one particular dorm at a university. Despite numerous attempts, the same results have never been found again, but given how quickly society jumped at the opportunity to explain one of the many complicated aspects of periods, this myth spread and stuck. More recent research—involving a lot more menstruating people—released in 2017 confirms that there is no truth to this. But it was too late: Period synching has become a routine—I'd even say cliché—part of pop culture.

There are so many examples of this, including episodes of *30 Rock* (2006–2013), *The Office* (2005–2013), and *Community* (2009–2015), where male characters remark on the fact that if the women in their inner circle spend a significant amount of time together, they will end up menstruating at the same time. In one of the very few episodes of *Sex and the City* (1998–2004) that even mentions periods, three of the women find that they are all menstruating at the same time. Unlike the other scenes mentioned above, this doesn't involve commentary from a man, but rather is used as a device to show the close friendship of these women.

In addition to the synching myth, there are plenty of examples where (typically male) characters allude to the fact that they are tracking their female friends' or colleagues' menstrual cycles, usually as a way to prepare themselves for the wrath of the women they must deal with on a regular basis. In an episode of *Community*, Abed Nadir (Danny Pudi) tells his study group that he has been charting the menstrual cycles of each of the women in his study group and adjusts the way he treats each of them as a result. Similarly, in an episode of *Friends* (1994–2004), when Chandler Bing (Matthew Perry) tries to guess what Rachel Green (Jennifer Aniston) has in her grocery bag, whispering to Joey Tribbiani (Matt LeBlanc) that he thought it was some sort of menstrual product, and Joey responds, "No, not for like another two weeks," demonstrating that he knows when she has her period. Finally, in an episode of *Murphy Brown* (1988–1998) Miles Silverberg (Grant Shaud) comments on his boss's behavior, asking whether it is "the eighteenth already"—letting the audience know that he also keeps track of her menstrual cycle.

WELCOME TO THE PERIOD PARADOX

If you think society's view of periods sounds like a no-win situation, you're right. On the one hand, we're expected to "suck it up"—just handle the pain and discomfort, and keep it to ourselves. After all, we know people think menstruation is gross and just part of being a woman, so no one wants to hear about it. On the other hand, there's also the perception that periods are *so* debilitating for women—mentally, physically, and emotionally—that we couldn't possibly hold positions of power or make high-level decisions as, say, an airplane pilot or politician. In other words, periods are simultaneously supposed to be so incapacitating that they're used to exclude us, *and* something so routine and insignificant that we're expected to just deal with it. This is what I call the period paradox—and yes, the idea is reinforced by pop culture.

The two episodes of *Roseanne* discussed earlier in this chapter clearly illustrate how the same show can perpetuate the period paradox. In one example, Dan gives D.J. permission to run away and scream in horror at the mere thought of his mother's period. In the other, Roseanne reassures Darlene that yes, it hurts, but it's normal—even "magical"—and doesn't need to change anything in her life.

An episode of the NBC sitcom *30 Rock*,

appropriately named "*TGS* Hates Women" acknowledges, then pokes fun at the period paradox. Responding to a negative review of the show based on its one-dimensional portrayal of women, head writer Liz Lemon (Tina Fey) explains that with the (male) costar of the show gone, the previous episode of *TGS* exclusively featured Jenna Maroney (Jane Krakowski). The scene then cuts to clips from that show, where Maroney played Amelia Earhart losing control of her plane because she got her period (leaving her unable to fly a plane), and then–Secretary of State Hillary Clinton exclaiming, "Let's nuke England!" because again, she had her period (leaving her unable to resist utilizing weapons of mass destruction). Cutting back to the *TGS* office, Lemon explains that those two examples are "an ironic reappropriation" of how women are typically shown in the media. She then goes on to say, "We should be elevating the way women are perceived in society," before stopping abruptly, clutching her abdomen, and yelling, "Oh, my period—you're all fired!" before collapsing backward. This reinforces the fact that whenever periods are shown on TV, it's done in a context that undermines women, regardless of the show's actual intentions.

SOMETHING'S MISSING

One of the only other times we see periods come up in television and films is when they are used in a pregnancy scare. For many people, a missed period is the first clue that they're pregnant—but of course, not everyone has a regular twenty-eight-day menstrual cycle, so the suspicion of pregnancy has to be confirmed by taking a test. This creates drama, building up to the point of either the character taking a pregnancy test or getting her period unexpectedly.

When Blanche Devereaux's period is late on an episode of *The Golden Girls*, she assumes that she is pregnant and, along with her roommates, starts planning for a later-in-life baby. But when she visits the doctor for confirmation, she finds out that not only is she not pregnant but that's also no longer likely: She is going through menopause. On *Sex and the City*, Samantha Jones (Kim Cattrall) hasn't gotten her period in nine weeks and suspects that she's "all dried up"—meaning, starting menopause—so she agrees to go on a date with a man she finds repulsive, assuming that no one else would be interested in her. She ends up getting her period while having sex with him—interestingly, the only time the groundbreaking show addressed the topic of period sex.

While first, last, and missed periods make the best plots, what's really missing from pop culture are realistic depictions of all the years in between puberty and menopause. An entire episode of *Broad City* (2014–) revolves around Abbi Abrams (Abbi Jacobson) getting her period while on an international flight. It's not her first, nor her last: It's one of many periods Abbi will get throughout her life. Regardless of how many apps you use to track your cycle or fertility, there are times when your period will be irregular and take you by surprise and, like Abbi, you may be left to improvise menstrual products. Another example of run-of-the-mill menstruation is a scene in *20th Century Women* (2016) when Abbie (Greta Gerwig) announces that she has her period at a dinner party. Another period period piece, it takes place in 1979, when this was an even more unusual topic of conversation than it is today. Abbie tries to get the rest of the people at the table to be comfortable with the word *menstruation* and makes each guest repeat it, with conviction. It's not a coincidence that the two examples of normal, non-milestone menstruation are the most recent: As we're becoming more comfortable—or at least more vocal—about periods, the more we'll see them pop up on-screen, leaving their mark on anyone who watches.

Resources

ORGANIZATIONS & NONPROFITS

All the organizations below are fighting the good fight for menstrual equity.

Society for Menstrual Cycle Research:
www.menstruationresearch.org

Blood Cycle Community:
www.bloodcyclecommunity.com

Take Charge. Period.:
www.takechargeperiod.org

Bleeders Are Leaders:
www.bleedersareleaders.com

Distributing Dignity:
www.distributingdignity.org

FLOW: www.helloflow.org

Girls Helping Girls. Period.:
www.girlshelpinggirlsperiod.org

Racket: www.weracket.com

Support the Girls:
www.isupportthegirls.org

Period. The Menstrual Movement:
www.period.org

Femme: www.respectfemme.org

Free the Tampons:
www.freethetampons.org

Days for Girls: www.daysforgirls.org

Irise International: www.irise.org.uk

MORE PERIOD-POSITIVE SITES AND ONLINE RESOURCES

Menstrual Health Hub: www.mhhub.org

Cycle Dork: www.cycledork.com

Museum of Menstruation: www.mum.org (This site is a little tricky to navigate, but the story behind it is fascinating. You can find Arielle Pardes's fantastic feature on the history of this museum on vice.com.)

Period!: www.period.media (This is an online magazine all about menstruation!)

Menstrual Hygiene Day:
www.menstrualhygieneday.org (Yes, there

is a day to celebrate menstrual hygiene—
it's May 28.)

BOOKS

New Blood: Third Wave Feminism and the Politics of Menstruation by Chris Bobel

Period Repair Manual: Natural Treatment for Better Hormones and Better Periods by Lara Briden

The Adventures of Toni the Tampon: A Period Coloring Book by Cass Clemmer

Out for Blood: Essays on Menstruation and Resistance by Breanne Fahs

Flow: The Cultural Story of Menstruation by Elissa Stein and Susan Kim

Periods Gone Public: Taking a Stand for Menstrual Equity by Jennifer Weiss-Wolf

Taking Charge of Your Fertility by Toni Weschler (Not just for people trying to get pregnant—an invaluable guide to how the reproductive system works.)

JOURNALISM

There has been some excellent coverage of periods in mainstream publications recently. Abigail Jones's writing for *Newsweek* stands out in particular:

"The Fight to End Period Shaming Is Going Mainstream." *Newsweek*, April 20, 2016.

"The Women Taking on Menstrual Equality." *Newsweek*, April 21, 2016.

"New York Terminates the Tampon Tax." *Newsweek*, July 21, 2016.

"Free Tampons and Pads Are Making Their Way to U.S. Colleges, High Schools, and Middle Schools." *Newsweek*, September 6, 2016.

"Cycles + Sex: Solving Lady-Part Problems, One Period at a Time." *Newsweek*, May 1, 2017.

"Periods, Policy and Politics: Menstrual Equity Is the New Thing." *Newsweek*, May 8, 2017.

"The Period Movement: Meet the Men Fighting to Stop Menstruation-Shaming in the Developing World." *Newsweek*, July 12, 2017.

"What's in a Tampon? Immigrant Dad's Mission to Transform Feminine Hygiene." *Newsweek*, July 24, 2017.

TED TALKS

Carine El Boustani, "On the Need to Speak Up About Period Pain," TEDxLAU

Diana Fabianova, "The Menstruation Taboo," TEDxBratislava
(Turn on the English subtitles for this one.)

Aditi Gupta and Tuhin Paul, "Can a Comic Book Overcome India's Menstruation Taboo?," TEDxBangalore

Annemarie Harant and Bettina Steinbrugger, "Breaking the Bloody Taboo," TEDxDonauinsel

Sophie Houser and Andy Gonzalez, "What Tampons Have to Do with Tech," TEDxYouth@Hewitt

Nancy Kramer, "Free the Tampons," TEDxColumbus

Sabrina Rubli, "Menstruation Matters," TEDxUW

GET INVOLVED—
CHANGE PUBLIC POLICY

If you live in a state that still taxes menstrual products as a luxury, contact your representatives and let them know this needs to change. Find your representatives here: www.usa.gov/elected-officials

Sign the petition to end the #TamponTax: www.change.org/m/end-the-tax -on-feminine-hygiene-products -notaxontampons

Period Equity: www.periodequity.org

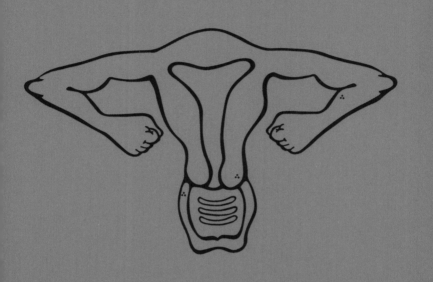

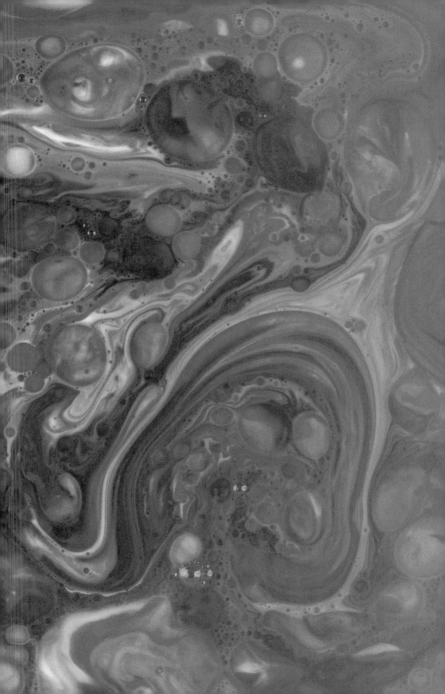

About the Authors

Arisleyda Dilone is a documentary film-maker, teacher, and writer.

Kate Farrell is an editor who lives in New York City.

Ann Friedman is a journalist and cultural critic. She is a columnist for *New York* magazine and the *Los Angeles Times*, and a contributing editor to *The Gentlewoman*. She cohosts the podcast *Call Your Girlfriend* with her friend Aminatou Sow and sends a popular weekly email newsletter. Find her work at annfriedman.com.

Madame Gandhi is an electronic music artist and activist based in Los Angeles. Having gained recognition as the former drummer for M.I.A. and as the famous free-bleeding runner at the 2015 London Marathon, Madame Gandhi now writes music that elevates and celebrates the female voice. madamegandhi.com

Santina Muha is a writer, actress, improviser, and comic. Originally from New Jersey, she now lives in Los Angeles. Follow her on Twitter @santinamuha.

Ingrid Nilsen is the personality and creative